# STREETS AHEAD

---

## An illustrated guide to the street names of Dunstable

---

Richard Walden

First published October 1999
by
The Book Castle
12 Church Street
Dunstable
Bedfordshire
LU5 4RU

ISBN  1 871199 54 9   (hardback)
ISBN  1 871199 59 x   (paperback)

Printed in Great Britain by Redwood Books, Trowbridge, Wiltshire

---

# THE AUTHOR

**Richard Walden** was born and educated in Wellingborough, Northants and has worked in local council administration for the past 33 years. He graduated in Public Administration from Leicester Polytechnic (De Montfort University) in 1971. He has lived in Dunstable since 1974 and worked for South Bedfordshire District and Luton Borough Councils. Since September 1985 he has been Town Clerk to Dunstable Town Council. He has extensive knowledge of the local area and is the author of recent editions of the Town Guide, pamphlets, leaflets and numerous newspaper and magazine articles about the town. He has been interviewed regularly on local radio about town affairs and has given many talks to local groups about the origins of the town's street names.

Richard Walden is actively involved in local community affairs. He is a member and Past President of the Rotary Club of Dunstable, Vice Chairman of the Ashton Schools Foundation, Hon Secretary to the Dunstable Access for All Committee, a member of Dunstable and District Local History Society and Dunstable Cricket Club as well a Trustee of several local charities. He is a member of the church family at St Augustine's in South Dunstable where he is a Sunday School teacher.

All royalties from "Streets Ahead" will support the work of the Friends of Dunstable Priory, of which Richard Walden was the founding Chairman.

# CONTENTS

**Introduction**..............................................5

The development of Dunstable from the mid 19th century; How streets are named; The meaning of the name "Dunstable"; the Dunstable Coat of Arms; the story of Dun The Robber.

**Chapter 1 - The Town Centre**.....................19

Watling Street (A5) High Street North and South; Icknield way (A505/B489) Church Street and West Street; The Priory; The Friary; Ashton Square; Queensway Hall and Quadrant Shopping Centre.

**Chapter 2 - West Central**..............................101

Bull Close Estate; Eleanors Cross; Prince Regent General Improvement Area; the Croft Estate.

**Chapter 3 - Priory Ward**.............................136

Englands Estate; Borough Farm Estate; Downside including Blows Downs.

**Chapter 4 - Beecroft**.................................167

Chiltern Road Estate; Beecroft Estate; Meteorological Station/Weatherby; Brewers Hill Road.

**Chapter 5 - North Dunstable**.....................195

Upper Houghton; French's Gate Estate; Station View Estate; Waterlows (Printers Way Estate); Northfields.

## Chapter 6 - West Dunstable.............................212
Meadway; Spoondell; Lancot Hill;
Whipsnade Road including California
and The Downs; The Avenue; Marina
Drive

## Chapter 7 - East Dunstable............................234
Luton Road; Legion Estate; Jeansway;
Ridgeway Avenue; Hadrian Estate;
Poynters Road Estate (Katherine Drive)

## Chapter 8 - Industrial Estates........................255
Dukeminster Estate (Bagshawes);
Boscombe Road (including Vauxhall
Motors and Renault/Commer); Eastern
Avenue; Woodside Estate.

## Chapter 9 - South West Dunstable......................266
Croft Golf Course Estate; Oldhill
Down; Stipers Hill; Index Printers;
Mentmore Crescent.

## Acknowledgements......................................300

## Index of Street Names................................301

## List of Subscribers..................................306

# Introduction

Since childhood I have been fascinated with the origins of the various street names in the locality in which I lived. This early interest was renewed when I came to study and work in the ancient market towns of Leicester and Northampton. Both have lost much of their medieval heyday but have still retained their original street patterns and, most importantly, the fascinating street names which reflected their past development.

On moving to Dunstable in the early 1970's I was therefore delighted to soon learn that, unusually, most of the town's street names had been selected for some specific reason. Dunstable's modern estates, in particular, had been spared the all too common anonymity of poets, painters, authors, birds and flowers found elsewhere. In Dunstable the name of a particular street reflected some aspect of the town's past; a former industry, local landmark or personality. As I explain shortly, the selection of road names generally falls to the developer or builder to initiate. In Dunstable's case the Council was itself often the developer, as the expansion of the town took place almost entirely in the era of great municipal housebuilding, and the Councillors took ( and still take) great care in the selection of particular names.

## The Development of Dunstable

Until the mid - nineteenth century Dunstable was a very small agricultural market town built almost exclusively around the four main streets made up of the Roman Watling Street and the even earlier Icknield Way, with only a very few courts and lanes leading off. The change came in the mid 19th century as the expanding hat and bonnet trade attracted workers from outlying villages and the arrival of the railways considerably aided the later attraction of major industry. In 1900, however, Dunstable was still a small Chilterns market town of approximately 4,500 persons with virtually no industry. Although foreign imports had placed the hat industry in decline, the principal local employment remained the cottage industry of straw plaiting associated with the local hat and bonnet trade which was now mainly established in nearby Luton. Development was, however, rapid in the early 20th century with the attraction of major printing and manufacturing companies, many of whom brought significant workforces with them. This development is graphically illustrated by reference to census returns during the past century as shown on the following page:

| Census Year | Population |
| --- | --- |
| 1901 | 5,157 |
| 1911 | 8,057 |
| 1921 | 8,889 |
| 1931 | 9,800 |
| 1939(Estimate) | 14,720 |
| 1951 | 17,254 |
| 1961 | 23,400 |
| 1971 | 31,790 |
| 1981 | 33,909 |
| 1991 | 33,350 |

Each major leap forward was a result of new industries locating to Dunstable, first printing and engineering works and later heavy truck manufacture which so dominated the town for all too brief a period. Homes were needed for the new workers and streets naturally had to be laid out to accommodate those houses.

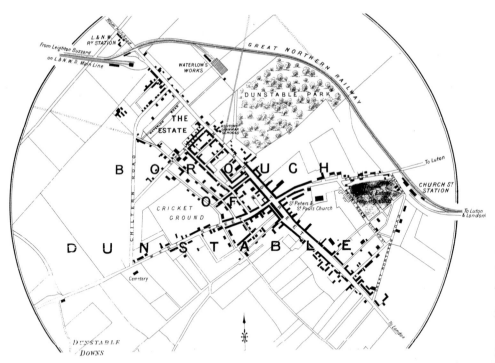

*A map of Dunstable published by the British Land Company in about 1910 showing two of their large housing estates, the first being the Englands Close Estate in 1880 (although most of the houses were built from 1905 onwards) and the second, the Bull Close Estate (Clifton Road area) in 1910. In 1861 the Company had purchased 248 acres of land in Dunstable in various plots but mainly in west Dunstable, which it proceeded to develop mainly through the employment of small local sub-contractors.*

Such was the wealth generated by these new industries that a major part of public policy during the 1930's was the encouragement of even more industry, as the resultant employment was seen as the antidote to the effects of the great Depression which generally had little impact upon Dunstable. The nearest most townsfolk came to the troubles facing much of the country was when one of the several unemployment or hunger protest marches passed through the town on the way to London.

If new industry was to be successfully attracted there was also a need to plan carefully how the town and its infrastructure should expand to meet the needs of the new labour forces. The Borough Council therefore appointed the eminent London consultant Town Planner, W R Davidge, in 1933 to advise on the appropriate strategy. Davidge envisaged a whole new network of housing and industrial estates linked by a new road pattern which took traffic away from the main crossroads which were already becoming congested.

*The street plan accompanying the 1939 Town Guide which includes W R Davidge's proposals for major new road building.*

*The cover of a brochure published by Dunstable Borough Council in 1939 to advertise the attractions of the town to prospective new industry.*

The second World War put paid to many of these plans but before its conclusion the Council published the far - sighted Plan for Dunstable, which attempted to guide how the town should be developed once peace had been restored. This Plan, and in particular its dramatic proposals for a new civic /entertainment/ shopping centre away from the main High Street, laid the foundations for the major developments in the north east quadrant, including the Queensway Hall and pedestrianised shopping centre which came to fruition in the late 1950's and early 1960's.

By the mid 1980's, however, economic recession and the decline of the traditional labour intensive printing processes had decimated Dunstable's main employers and new policies of regeneration had to be developed. The "brown field" sites left by the old industries are being redeveloped for a mixture of uses including housing. The illustrations in this book are testimony to some of this rapid change but it is clear that, as the pace of regeneration picks up, many of the present day photographs will soon become outdated.

Accordingly, as well as attempting to explain some of the reasons for selecting the names of those streets, this work and its illustrations may therefore be viewed as an introduction to the principal economic and social trends affecting the nation during the 20th century, many of which can be found in microcosm in the development of Dunstable. It is a facet of the town's recent past which perhaps has not previously received sufficient recognition.

## Acknowledgements

My interest in the origins of the town's street names was rekindled when the Editor of the Dunstable Gazette, John Buckledee, asked me to expand upon some original research for the Dunstable Museum Trust by Mrs Margaret Lines. This work appeared in a series of articles in The Gazette from 1992-5. Since then I have been very grateful to the countless numbers of former Council colleagues, developers and other individuals who have very kindly helped with my researches. I am particularly grateful for the considerable help I have received from Ray Barlow and Omer Roucoux without whose tireless efforts this work would not have been possible. Many of the suggested origins of names remain conjectural or refer to local hearsay and I am sure further revision will prove necessary in the future. I must also record a debt of gratitude to Trevor Wood, who has designed this work with great skill and put up with my foibles with much patience.

I am also grateful to the Town Mayor and members of Dunstable Town Council for their help and support throughout. The Town Council has also kindly consented to the reproduction of photographs and documents from the Council archives.

Where photos have come from other sources, the appropriate acknowledgement is included and here again I must mention one person, local photographer Bruce Turvey, who has very kindly devoted much time and effort to assisting me with appropriate illustrations for which I am deeply appreciative. I must also mention Philip Heley and Bill Stevens, who assisted enormously in compiling a current photo record of every town street. Space finally allowed only a fraction to be reproduced here but the remainder will, I am sure become, an important local archive.

*Grove House, a former Georgian coaching inn, now the headquarters of Dunstable Town Council, where several of the original paintings contained in this book are displayed.*

## How Streets are named

Contrary to popular opinion, Councils do not have the final say in the naming of streets. Locally the South Bedfordshire District Council has adopted the permissive powers of the Town Improvement Clauses Act 1847 (later incorporated in the Public Health Act 1875) which empowers them to name and number streets in their area. District Councils also have a specific power under Section 21 of the Public Health Amendments Act 1907, to alter the name of a street or to name an un-named street. An Order to give effect to such a decision must be advertised and any aggrieved person may appeal against it to the Magistrates Court before the Order is finally made.

The owner of a development has a right of appeal to the Magistrates Court against any decision of the District Council to give particular names to the streets in that development. In considering an appeal against a proposal from the District Council the Magistrates must ensure the grounds are "reasonable". For example it could be properly argued that a particular name could be confusing especially to the emergency or postal services if a similar name existed close by.

It is extremely unlikely that Magistrates would be able to sustain an appeal solely on the grounds that someone did not like the name proposed and would prefer one which better reflected the heritage of the area. The fact that so many names in Dunstable do reflect the area probably testifies to the persuasive powers of successive District Council members and officers.

Local Councils, such as Dunstable Town Council, have no direct powers with respect to the naming of streets. However we are fortunate that locally the South Bedfordshire District Council has always adopted a policy of seeking the views and advice of the relevant town or parish council before considering any notified street name. This in turn has allowed the Town Council to liaise with local interested groups and individuals as well as the developer to achieve a mutually acceptable name to put to the District Council. This system generally works well with the District Council (usually acting through its Chief Building Control Officer) tending to adopt the role of an unbiased mediator between the views of a builder/ developer and other interested parties such as the Town Council. Within the main body of this work there are, however, unfortunately several examples where the developers' suggestions prevailed despite the Town Council's views, as to continue to object could well have been deemed "unreasonable".

# Why are Street Names important ?

Many people may feel that it matters not a jot whether the street in which they live is named after a bird or some ancient field name or local dignitary. I could not disagree more wholeheartedly. In today's ever changing society and particularly in today's Dunstable with its increasingly transient population and the ever present scourge of through traffic and heavy lorries, we should do everything in our power to seek to engender a sense of identity amongst our local community. This is vital if we are to have regard for our town and our fellow citizens. An important element of this is to remember and to respect our shared past heritage. Great effort has been expended in the past to reflect that heritage in the selection of local street names and if in any small way this publication promotes an appreciation of that effort, then all the countless hours of research will have been worthwhile.

# The meaning of the name "Dunstable"

Dunstable, or "Dunstaple" as it was usually written in the past, is derived from two Anglo - Saxon words, "Dun" meaning a hill or Down and "Staple" meaning market. So Dunstable is quite literally "The market by the Downs". This reflects the fact that the modern town was established by Henry I some time before 1109 on the site of a former Roman posting station. The King later regularised the markets which were being held at the crossroads of Watling Street and Icknield Way and granted local control over the market to the Priory of St Peter in the town's first Charter in 1131.

These events are depicted in the town's armorial bearings shown below:

The present-day version of the Dunstable Arms was adopted by Dunstable Borough Council in 1865 pursuant to special privileges granted to it by a Royal Charter of Queen Victoria in 1864. These special rights were passed on to Dunstable Town Council in 1985.

The extended version of the Arms shown above was registered with the College of Arms on 5th June 1865. The full heraldic description is "Argent, a Pile Sable, charged with Ring and Staple, on Bordure, Engralid of the Third". The Latin inscription means "Justice for All".

The Arms show a market post and staple with gold ring attached depicting that Dunstable's ancient market was granted under royal authority. The design is derived from an original Coat of Arms granted by Henry I in 1135 to Dunstable Priory, a version of which is still in use by the Priory Church of St Peter today.

*Sixty feet above the altar of the Priory Church is this figure, probably carved about 1480, with a shield which must be the earliest example of the Arms of Dunstable. (OR)*

# The Story of "Dun The Robber"

A far more colourful but unproven alternative version of the origin of the name "Dunstaple" comes from the legend of Dun The Robber. The story goes that before Henry I established his new town around the Watling Street and Icknield Way crossroads the area was plagued by a band of robbers led by one Dun or *Dunna* or *Dunning*. To tempt them into the open the King had a stake planted at the crossroads and fixed to it his gold ring, held in place by a staple as a challenge to Dun to steal it. Dun accomplished this successfully despite the King's guard but, after further adventures, was eventually captured and executed. The new town which followed shortly after these events was named after "Dun's Staple".

DUNA, the Anglo-Saxon owner of the present Site of DUNSTABLE, with the Pillar, or STAPOL, erected as a mark of ownership.

*A conjectural drawing of Dun by Worthington G Smith, the original of which hangs in the Mayor's Parlour at Grove House.*

14

Although this story was once accepted as factual by generations of local schoolchildren, there is no contemporary evidence that any of the events actually took place. The earliest recorded mention of Dun is in the Priory Annals in 1290, some 200 years after the events are supposed to have taken place. The bulk of the story, however, seems to derive from the following poem written in the Priory Church Register in 1600 by John Willis:

"By Houghton Regis, there, where Watlinge Streete
Is cross'd by Icknell way, once grew a wood
With bushes thick orespred; a coverte meete
To harbour such as lay in waite for blood,
There lurkte of ruffians bolde an hideous route
Whose captaine was one Dunne, of courage Stoute.

"No travailer almost coulde passe that way
But either he was wounded, rob'd, or kil'd
By that leude crewe, which there in secreete lay:
With murthers, theftes, and rapes, their hands were fil'd,
What booties ere they tooke, ech had his share;
Thus yeere by yeere they liv'd without all care.

"At last King Henrie, first king of that name,
Towards the northern partes in progresse rode;
And hearinge of those great abuses, came
Unto the thicket where the theeves abode;
Who on the comminge of the kinge did flie
Each to his house, or to his friende did hie.

"Wherefore the kinge, such mischiefes to prevent,
The wood cut downe; the way all open layde
That all trew men, which that way rode or wente,
Of sodaine sallyes might be lesse affrayde;
And might descrie theire danger ere it came,
An so by wise foresighte escape the same.

"This done, he rear'd a poull both houge and longe
In that roade-highway, where so manie passe;
And in the poul let drive a staple stronge,
Whereto the kinge's own ringe appendant was;
And caus'd it to be publisht that this thinge,
Was done to see what thiefe durst steale the ringe.

"Yet for all that, the ringe, was stol'n away,
Which, when it came to learned Beauclark's eare,
By skylful arte to finde, he did assay
Who was the thiefe, and first, within what shyre
His dwellinge was, which this bould act had done,
And found it to be Bedfordshire, anon.

"Next in what hundred off that shyre might dwell
This vent'rous wighte, Kinge Henrie caste to find;
And upon Mansfield Hundred, straight it fell,
Which being founde, he after bent his minde
to learn the parish, and by like skylll tride
That he in Houghton Regis did abide.

"Lastlie, the parish knowne, he further soughte
To find the verie house where he remaynde;
And by the preceptes of his arte he toughte;
That by one widow Dun he was retayned;
The widowe's house was searched, so wil'd the kinge,
And with her sonne was founde, staple and ringe.

"Thus Beauclarke by his arte, founde out the thiefe;
A lustie tall younge man of courage good,
Which of the other ruffians was the Chiefe;
That closlie lurked in that waylesse wood.
Then Dunne, this captain thiefe, the widowe's sonne,
Was hanged for the feates which he had donne.

"And where the thicket stoode, the kinge did build
A market towne for saulfetie of all those
Which travail'd that way, that it might them yielde
A sure refuge from all thievishe foes;
And there king Henrie, of his great bountie,
Founded a church, a schole, and priorie.

"And for that Dunne, before the woode was downe,
Had there his haunte, and thence did steale away
The staple and the ring, thereof the towne
Is called Dunstaple untill this day;
also in armes, that corporation,
The staple and the ringe give thereupon."

*A copy of John Willis's poem of Dun the Robber in the Parish Register, drawn by Worthington G Smith in 1909.*

# KEY MAP

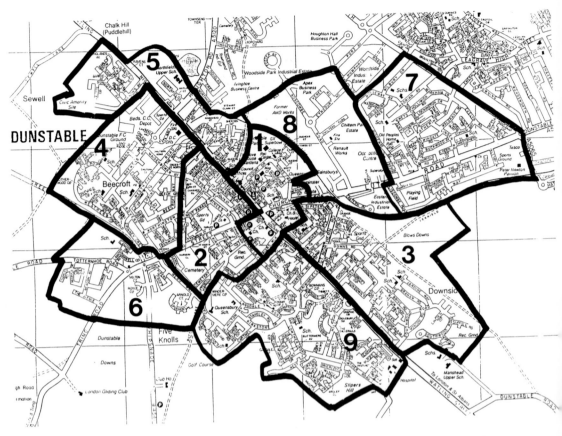

1. Town Centre

2. West Central

3. Priory Ward

4. Beecroft

5. North Dunstable

6. West Dunstable

7. Icknield Ward

8. Industrial Estates

9. South West Dunstable

# Chapter 1 - THE TOWN CENTRE

Until the late 19th century, Dunstable had principally comprised the four main crossroads, formed by the prehistoric Icknield Way (A505 and B489) and the Roman Watling Street (A5), together with a few courtyards and lanes leading off them. This comparatively small area remained the commercial and trading heart of the town. It was not until the late 1950's and early 1960's that development took place away from the four main roads. It was then that the local Borough Council undertook or initiated the major expansion of a pedestrianised shopping precinct, civic centre, court, library and college. In the mid 1970's a further shopping development in the south west quadrant replaced the former Chapel Walk and St Mary's Street.

The great period of growth symbolised by these developments was sadly short-lived. The parallel collapse of the town's dominant heavy truck manufacturing base due to overcapacity in the European truck market and the fall off in demand for military vehicles at the end of the Cold War, as well as major printing works due to the impact of modern technology in the late 1980's, had a dramatic effect on the town's economy. This was compounded by the Secretary of State's decision in 1987 to allow the appeal of Tesco Stores against the refusal by the South Bedfordshire District Council to grant planning permission for a new food superstore on the edge of the town in Skimpot Road. Two years later a similar appeal by Sainsbury's for an edge of town superstore in Boscombe Road was also successful, so robbing the town centre of its two main general stores. Competition from other newer and larger centres and the failure of successive central governments to address the overriding problem of excessive volumes of through traffic, especially heavy lorries, all conspired to reduce the attraction of the town centre as a shopping and leisure venue.

The response of the local authorities to this challenge has been the adoption, after a period of extensive consultation, of the 1997 Town Centre Strategy. This plans to significantly enhance the appearance of the town and implement medium term traffic management measures until Government comes forward with permanent traffic relief. There are already signs that these measures will encourage private investors to come to Dunstable to help once more improve the town's shopping and leisure "offer". The changes proposed are already in the process of being implemented and many of the street scenes included in this book will have changed dramatically by the time of publication.

*A much re-produced drawing by Worthington G Smith (see Worthington Road) of the scene at the crossroads in 1885. The original drawing now hangs in the Mayor's Parlour in the Town Council Offices at Grove House.*

*An aerial photograph of the main crossroads showing High Street South and The Square in the foreground. Taken in July 1972, several important changes will be noticed from the scene today. In the foreground The Square is still an area for general car parking but was soon to disappear with the construction of the various raised flowerbeds still in evidence today. Middle Row is clearly recognisable but Ashton Street is still an ordinary thoroughfare but with traffic operating in the opposite direction from The Square to West Street. This led to frequent "rat runs" by vehicles seeking to avoid the crossroads traffic lights and the flow was reversed in 1975. On the left of the picture the buildings in Chapel Walk and St Mary's Street have been substantially cleared but the area is still a temporary car park and the modern Ashton Square shopping development has not yet been started. On the right hand side of the picture above Priory Gardens can clearly be seen the site of the recently demolished Index Printing Works in Church Walk. This site will shortly be developed for the Priory Health Centre.(Aerofilms)*

# HIGH STREET NORTH

Originally known as North Street, with its neighbour, High Street South, it has been the town's main street for centuries. Now part of the modern A5 Trunk Road, the High Street was originally part of the great Roman Road leading from Dover to North Wales and later known as Watling Street. The High Street was often referred to as Watling Street in times past and the section north of the junction with Houghton Road was still officially referred to by that name into the 1930's. The section north of Albion Street was known as Upper Houghton and was transferred into the Borough from Houghton Regis in 1907.

We do not know by what name the Romans called the road, the name "Watling" only appearing for the first time in 886 AD and is probably derived from the name of a local chieftain.

*One of the oldest views of Dunstable High Street taken about 1870. The dominant building on the right is the old Market House which was purchased from Queen Victoria by the Dunstable Borough Council in 1866 and used as the Town Hall for meetings and the local Court. The Clocktower shown in the photograph was erected in 1869 but the whole building was destroyed by fire in 1879. It was replaced by the fondly remembered Victorian Town Hall in 1880. Also of interest in the photograph is the large number of steps leading to the front doors of the properties on the right of the photograph. These clearly show how various road improvements and resurfacings over the years have increased the road levels we see today. The photograph is taken from an original print in the Mayor's Parlour in Grove House.*

*High Street North in the 1870's looking south towards the crossroads. The picture is taken from outside Grove House and the building on the right on the site of the present Bingo Club was Coopers Hat Factory which was later brought into multiple occupation housing use. The conditions inside had deteriorated to such an extent by 1932 that, on the advice of the Medical Officer of Health, the Council issued a Closing Order and the building was demolished. (DG)*

*High Street North in the 1870's looking north showing Nicholas Lane and the White Hart Inn on the right with the horse and carriage outside. Further along the street the facade of the Old Sugar Loaf is clearly visible. (DG)*

The same scene as in the previous picture taken about 1890. Part of the building on the right is now in use as the town's first Post Office which later moved to the premises now occupied by the Department of Social Security on the opposite side of the road in 1912. The building has now been replaced by Barclays Bank. (DG)

High Street North looking northwards from the crossroads in about 1900. The large building on the right is the Red Lion Hotel, one of Dunstable's ancient Coaching Inns which was demolished as part of the Church Street road widening scheme in 1964.

*The Town Hall next to the Crown Inn in about 1900. Built in 1880 the Town Hall was demolished in July 1966 and is now the site of the Woolwich Building Society.*

*High Street North in about 1900 looking southwards from the junction with Manchester Place - note the condition of the road surface!*

*The scene in High Street North on the arrival of the first trial omnibus service from London to Dunstable in 1902. (DG)*

*The scene outside the Town Hall in 1910 on the occasion of the death of King Edward VII. The Union Flag is flying at half mast and the procession is moving off to a memorial service in the Priory Church. The gradual improvement in the road surface over the past 5 photographs is clearly visible. (DG)*

*Scottish marchers protesting about cuts in unemployment benefit pass through Dunstable in November 1936. Dunstable was at the time one of the main transport routes into London and saw several major protests during the 1930's. The entrance to Nicholas Lane can be seen on the right next to the premises of Allcorn. The Old Sugar Loaf in the distance has by now gained the large replica Sugar Loaf above the portico which we see today. (DG)*

*A happier scene outside the Town Hall on the occasion of the Coronation of King George VI in 1937. (DG)*

*An aerial view from the late 1930's clearly showing the wide and straight Watling Street Roman Road which now forms High Street North and South. Grove House is bottom left looking southwards. In the top right the town ends with the "new" developments in Periwinkle Lane and Garden Road. (DG)*

*The Mayor of Dunstable, Councillor A E Sharman takes the salute as a Bren Gun Carrier passes the rostrum outside the Town Hall as part of a parade to mark Dunstable's War Weapons Week in March 1941. To the left of the Mayor wearing the wig and gown is the Town Clerk, Mr A D (Don) Harvey (see Harvey Road). (DG)*

*Heavy snows in January 1950. The Union Cinema is on the right and its smaller neighbour, the Palace Cinema which was demolished in the mid 1960's.(BT)*

*Traffic splashing through the aftermath of a storm in High Street North in May 1951. Various parts of Dunstable have been frequently subjected to flash flooding due to the incapacity of the storm water sewerage system. A problem which has only been finally solved in 1999 after a programme of major sewerage improvement works by Anglian Water. (DG)*

*Carnival day in June 1954 showing the stalls of the town market on the west side between West Street and Albion Street. (BT)*

*The queue of cars following the Coronation Carnival procession in High Street North in June 1953. (BT)*

*Traffic struggles through a blizzard in January 1955. (DG)*

*An aerial view of the crossroads and High Street North in 1955 showing the Maltings and other outbuildings to the rear of properties in High Street North on the site of the present Quadrant Shopping Centre. At the very top of the picture can be seen the Wartime huts which stood roughly on the site of the Queensway Hall. (LM/DG)*

*An aerial view of High Street North in 1961 showing in the centre the Dunstable Grammar School (now Ashton Middle School). In the bottom left of the picture can be seen the terraced houses in Union Street which were demolished in the late 1960's and have now been replaced by a modern housing scheme. In the background is the Waterlows Printing Works fronted by its impressive office block and distinctive clocktower. On the right of the picture can be seen the short-lived bandstand in Grove House Gardens. Behind it the area of Park Estate has not yet been brought into public use and later development as part of the Dunstable Recreation Centre (now Dunstable Leisure Centre).(LM/DG)*

*Market Day outside the Town Hall in June 1960. (EM)*

*Another scene of the market stalls, this time not in use, during a snow storm in January 1963. (BT)*

*High Street North in 1985 looking southwards from the junction with Albion Street. Barriers have now appeared at the pedestrian crossing near the Sugar Loaf and pedestrians are deterred from crossing the road by the Quadrant Shopping Centre by raised flowerbeds. These proved unsuccessful and were replaced by further railings in 1991. (BCC).*

*This section of High Street North north of Union Street was part of the parish of Houghton Regis until the extension of the Dunstable Borough boundary in 1907. Prior to that this area was known as "Upper Houghton". The distinctive property in the distance on the right is The Tower House, the residence of Mr J T Dales of Dales Dubbin Company (see Dale Road).*

*An unusual view of High Street North looking northwards in July 1995 taken from a specially erected surveying tower deployed by South Bedfordshire District Council to help determine the locations of the CCTV cameras installed later that year.*

*High Street North looking towards the crossroads in 1997. The dominance of the motor vehicle and measures taken to control it, have significantly changed the character of the town's high street seen in the earlier photographs.*

# HIGH STREET SOUTH

Originally known as South Street.

*High Street South in about 1876 showing a group of workers or "hands" in front of a hat factory which later became "The Grey House" a residence of the Bagshawe Family (see Dukeminster Estate). The property is now the Downtown Café. Beyond it the buildings of Montpelier Chambers, Cart Almshouses and Chew's House are largely unchanged today. (DG)*

*High Street South showing, on the right, the entrance to Wood Street and beyond the Saracen's Head.*

*High Street South looking northwards from the junction with King Street in about 1900.*

*High Street South looking southwards from an old postcard posted in 1913. The first property containing Bigg's Milliners and Freeman, Hardy and Willis was demolished in 1963 as part of the Church Street road widening scheme.*

*High Street South about 1930 showing the Saracen's Head in the centre. (BS)*

*High Street South looking northwards in the 1930's showing the properties in Middle Row.*

*Flooding in High Street South outside the Saracen's Head in May 1936. The cattle pens of the cattle market on The Square are visible on the left.*

*The Greyhound Public House at the junction of High Street South and Great Northern Road in the 1930's.(DG)*

*Two watercolours by Thomas Fisher in about 1812 showing important buildings in High Street South - (Top) Priory House with adjoining it, Munt and Brown's Hat Factory. Although the Hat Factory has been long demolished part of the front wall has been retained as the boundary to Priory Gardens and the two ground floor windows shown here are clearly distinguishable today. (Bottom) Jane Cart's Almshouses. These paintings are part of a series purchased by Dunstable Town Council following a public subscription organised by the Dunstable & District Local History Society in 1992. The paintings now hang in the Council Chamber at Grove House.*

*A view of High Street South from The Square looking towards High Street North taken in July 1995 as part of surveying work before the installation of CCTV cameras.*

*A montage view of High Street South in 1995. The contractors in the centre of the photograph are about to install the CCTV cameras. Whilst on the left of the photograph in front of "The Friars" only one of the trees seen as an avenue in earlier photographs now remains.*

*Older Dunstablians will immediately recognise 4 of the most well known shops in the town on the eastern side of High Street South. This photograph was taken in January 1953. The first 2 properties were demolished in 1963 as part of the Church Street road widening scheme (BT)*

*High Street South junction with Church Street in 1929. In the days before traffic lights, the narrow width of Church Street at this junction required the permanent presence of a police constable on point duty.(DG)*

*An aerial view of High Street South in about 1961 showing, in the centre, the Priory Church and to its left the row of cottages in Church Walk (now part of the Church Close car park). In front of these and behind the premises now occupied by Moore's Department Store is the Index Printing Works. In the background properties on the north side of Church Street are starting to be demolished for the road widening scheme but the Quadrant Shopping Centre has not yet been implemented. In the top left corner the new Dunstable College, which opened in 1961, is nearing completion at the end of Kingsway whilst in the background the impact of the huge Vauxhall Motor works on the town is aptly demonstrated. (DG)*

# THE SQUARE

Officially not a square at all but a long triangle adjoining High Street South and extending from Friars Walk to Middle Row. For centuries The Square was the site for markets and public meetings. The cattle market closed in 1955 and the traditional "Statty Fair" was moved to an off-street car park in 1976. The general market was relocated back to the site in October 1998.

*The Wesleyan Chapel on The Square in about 1900. Built in 1845 this was the second Chapel on the site; the first, which was built in 1831, was destroyed by fire in 1844. The second Chapel and the Wesleyan Day School (see Graham Road) were also destroyed by fire in 1908.*

*A huge crowd gathers to witness the laying of the Foundation Stone of the present Methodist Church on 31st May 1909. In the background can be seen the houses of Chapel Walk. (DG)*

*The present Methodist Church taken in 1990.*

*The Square in about 1915.*

*Cattle Market at The Square in May 1947. (DG)*

*"Statty Fair" in September 1947. (DG)*

*Prime Minister Sir Alec Douglas Home addresses a large crowd at The Square on 7th October 1964 during an election rally. (BT)*

*Large crowds still gather on The Square each year for the now traditional Christmas Carols Ceremony. This shows the scene in December 1992 with the Town Mayor, Mrs Joan Goodall, at the front of the rostrum. (MP)*

*The scene at The Square in the late 1990's when buses and taxis dominated the town's traditional meeting place, prior to the relocation of the general market to this site in October 1998.*

*May 1999 and the general market has been relocated to the Square.*

DUNSTABLE TOWN CLOCK. MARKET SQUARE.

FJP 01-99

*A view by Mr Frank Porthouse of how his design for a new Market Cross and Clock will provide a new identifying feature for the town by the year 2000.*

# WEST STREET

One of the four main crossroads of Dunstable which, together with Church Street (previously called East Street), comprises part of the prehistoric Icknield Way which joined the Ridgeway to Peddars Way in Norfolk. As late as the 1930's the Borough Council, in official correspondence with the Government, was still referring to West Street as "The Icknield Way".

*West Street in about 1900 looking from the junction with Victoria Street to the crossroads. The large building on the left later became Moreton House School; the site is now occupied by a modern office development.*

*The scene in about 1910 looking from the junction with Princes Street towards the crossroads.*

*West Street Windmill in about 1900. The Mill was built in 1839 but the sails were removed in 1908 when it continued in use as a steam mill until the second World War. In 1948 it was officially renamed as "Training Ship Lionel Preston" as the Headquarters of the Dunstable Sea Cadet Unit named in honour of their Founder Admiral Sir Lionel Preston who had retired to Dunstable in 1935. (LM)*

*Shops on the south side of West Street looking from Cross Street West (see St Mary's Gate) towards the Red Lion Hotel at the crossroads in about 1920.*

*West Street in about 1920 looking in the opposite direction from the crossroads westwards.*

*West Street at the junction with High Street North in about 1930. The first properties in Middle Row have been demolished as part of a road improvement scheme but the "new corner" shop, Keep's Newsagents, has not yet been adapted to include its familiar shop windows (now Taylors Estate Agents).*

*Cottages on the north side of West Street in 1972 shortly before their demolition to make way for the car park which now adjoins St Mary's RC Church. (JB)*

*West Street Christian Centre in about 1970. Built in 1847-8 as the West Street Baptist Church the front extensions seen today were added in 1984 to accommodate the Pilgrim Christian School. (JB)*

*St Mary's Roman Catholic Church (more correctly the Church of Our Lady Immaculate) which was built in 1964 at the rear of the first Catholic Church which had been opened in 1936 and is now the St Mary's Social Club (JB)*

*Council maisonettes and houses at the junction of West Street and Drovers Way shortly after their completion in the late 1950's. (SBDC)*

*West Street from the junction with Matthew Street looking towards the crossroads in February 1964. The Red Lion Hotel has now been demolished but the old Westminster Bank which adjoined it has not yet been redeveloped as the new Nat West Bank Centre.(BT)*

*Cemetery Lodge (now demolished) in September 1973 showing the start of the construction of the new roundabout junction with Chiltern Road. (LM/DG)*

*The completed new junction with Chiltern Road in early 1975. (BT)*

*Scenes of West Street in 1995. A new improvement scheme is proposed for late 1999 and the scene is likely to change radically again.*

# CHURCH STREET

Originally known as East Street, the change reflected the common usage for the street which contains Dunstable's most important building, the Priory Church of St Peter. The present church was originally the nave of the chapel of St Peter's Priory, the majority of which was demolished after the dissolution of the Monasteries by Henry VIII. Church Street was only wide enough, at its western end, to accommodate one line of traffic. This was a major point of congestion and the regrettable solution was that the carriageway was widened considerably during the early 1960's, resulting in a loss of many of the town's best loved landmarks including the White Horse Inn and Red Lion Hotel.

*Church Street looking east in about 1900. Sadly, all the buildings on the left-hand side have been demolished as part of the 1960's road widening scheme. The first building on the left is the White Horse Inn which stood approximately where the entrance to Broadwalk is today. Outside the Inn, but not shown in this picture, was a mounting stone which was saved by local historian Mr John Lunn and placed within the grounds of Beecroft Lower school, where he was at the time Headmaster.(BS)*

*Church Street looking west from the junction with Priory Road. The railings of the Priory Churchyard wall were removed during the second World War.*

*The narrow section of Church Street at its junction with High Street in 1929 showing the now demolished Red Lion Hotel. (LM/DG)*

*The First and Last Inn in the early 1900's. (LM/DG)*

*The lower section of Church Street in the late 1920's. In the centre picture on the left can be seen the row of cottages which once stood in front of Ashton St Peter Lower School. The entrance into Church Close on the right is hard to distinguish.(BCC)*

*The Royal British Legion Remembrance Parade about to enter Church Close from Church Street on 13th November 1938. (LM/DG)*

*The Old Contemptibles about to leave Church Street into High Street North during the Civic Service Parade on 30th May 1954. (BT)*

*Road improvement works beneath the Church Street Railway Bridge in the mid 1960's showing the Dunstable Town Railway Station which closed to passengers in 1965. (DG)*

*Inadequate capacity in the town's storm water drainage was the cause of frequent flash flooding beneath the Church Street Railway Bridge during periods of heavy rainfall. These pictures were taken in May and August 1988 respectively. (DG)*

The problem of flooding in Church Street was finally resolved in 1996 when Anglian Water constructed a huge deep shaft storm water storage tank in front of the Dukeminster Estate with capacity to hold storm water during periods of heavy rainfall. The work was a major undertaking and involved the use of substantial heavy plant. The photograph of the large crane was taken from the Dukeminster Estate and shows in the background the Eastern Avenue Industrial Estate with Blows Down behind it. (Anglian Water).

*A view of Church Street showing the First and Last Inn from the top of the crane constructing the storm water drainage in September 1996.(Anglian Water)*

*Church Street in 1995 showing how Quadrant House office block, built in 1965, dominates the street scene. Also of interest on the left hand side is a bus bearing the short lived logo "Dunstable Bus" operated by Luton and District Transport before the company's acquisition , initially by The Shires and later by Arriva.*

*At the time of writing (1999) Quadrant House is vacant but it still affords the opportunity for unusual aerial views of the town. This Montage view looking up West Street towards Dunstable Downs was taken in 1995.*

*An unusual view of Church Street from the crossroads taken by a surveying tower used to determine the locations for the installation of CCTV cameras.*

# CHURCH CLOSE

Originally known as either Church Close or "Priory Close". Church Close was formally adopted in 1952 when the car park was first provided, in order to avoid confusion with Priory Road and so misdirect drivers.

*The west front of the Priory Church of St Peter seen from Church Close in about 1900, which has been referred to as "the architectural gem of Bedfordshire". For over 800 years the Priory has been at the heart of town affairs and in 1533 hosted an event which changed history when Archbishop Cranmer declared the annulment of the marriage between Henry VIII and Katherine of Aragon. This eventually led to the split from the Roman Catholic Church and the declaration of Henry as Head of the Church of England in 1535.*

*A montage view of Church Close, the Priory Church, Priory Meadow and the Church Close Car Park which replaced the buildings seen on the next page. Taken from the top of Quadrant House in 1995.*

*Sergeant Major O'Dell leads the Dunstable Grammar School Cadet Unit at the head of the Civic Service Parade in Church Close in July 1934. (DG)*

*The view from the Priory Church Tower in about 1900 showing the Town Hall in the centre with Church Walk in the foreground.*

*The same view taken from the Church Tower in the early 1980's. (OR)*

# CHURCH WALK

An ancient footpath leading from the crossroads to the Priory Church and later through the churchyard into what is now Priory Road.

*The view of the section of Church Walk from Priory Road through the Church Yard in about 1910.*

*Wedding sightseers waiting for the bride's arrival outside the Priory Church in September 1955, showing the cottages in Church Walk in the background. (BT)*

*Church Walk in about 1930 looking towards the Priory Church.*

*The same view taken in the late 1980's.*

# ASHTON SQUARE

Originally named Ashton Street. The Ashton Almshouses previously stood at the corner of West Street and were relocated in Bull Pond Lane after demolition to make way for the shopping development of the early 1970's. The road was renamed "Square" when partially pedestrianised as part of the redevelopment.

*The Ashton Almshouses at the junction of Ashton Street (as it then was) and West Street in about 1812 painted by Thomas Fisher. The Town Stocks and Whipping Post stand in front of the Almshouses wall. Public flogging for comparatively minor offences ceased in 1850.*

*The Ashton Almshouses in about 1890 showing some of the women residents wearing their distinctive bonnets. The Stocks have by now disappeared. (DG)*

*The rear of Middle Row properties fronting Ashton Street in about 1970. (JB)*

*The same scene taken in 1985 after completion of the pedestrianisation scheme. (BCC)*

*Ashton Square looking south and north respectively in 1985. (BCC)*

# BERNARD CLOSE

Named after the developer, Bernard Estates. It has been suggested that the name may also have come from Bernard Street in London where local developer, Mr T C Flory, first met his wife.

# BROADWALK

A suitable name for the widest section of the pedestrianised Quadrant Shopping Centre.

*Broadwalk in 1985 with the distinctive, but much disliked, Quadrant Clock. (BCC)*

*The same view in 1990.*

# CHAPEL WALK

Originally the town end of Cemetery Lane which has been absorbed into the St Mary's Gate car park but remains a right of way between the Methodist Church and the Wilkinson's store. Previously called Havewycke and then Hollowick Lane, the "Chapel" refers to the Ebenezer Baptist Chapel which replaced a much older place of worship in 1849. The section of the car park nearest to Bull Pond Lane is now known officially as "Chapel Walk Car Park".

*An aerial view of the western half of the town centre in July 1972. Chapel Walk can be seen on the right but only two buildings, the Baptist Chapel and the Queens Head Public House, have not been demolished. The latter will shortly would shortly suffer the same fate to make way for the car park to serve the new Sainsbury's Ashton Square development. (Aerofilms)*

*The Foresters Arms Public House in St Mary's Street in about 1970. This was one of the last properties to be demolished to make way for the new Sainsbury's car park. (JB)*

*Chapel Walk in 1985 has been retained as a pedestrian right of way between the Methodist Church and the Sainsbury's (now Wilkinson's) Store. (BCC)*

# COURT DRIVE

The new road constructed between Queensway and Kingsway in 1962 provided access to the Dunstable Magistrates Court, opened in July 1963. The Justices previously sat in the Town Hall in High Street North whilst the Juvenile Bench sat in a beautiful Tudor-panelled room in Grove House now occupied by the Office of the Superintendent Registrar.

*The children's play area in Grove House Gardens seen from Court Drive in 1964.*

*Dunstable Magistrates Court in 1986. In 1999 the Lord Chancellor confirmed the decision of the Bedfordshire Magistrates Committee to close the Dunstable Magistrates Court and to transfer its business to Luton, so ending 130 years of the administration of local justice in Dunstable.*

*Two views of Dunstable Market at the short-lived Queensway Market Square taken from the balcony of the Queenway Hall in March 1990. Showing at the top the view towards Grove House and (bottom) the view across Court Drive towards Dunstable Leisure Centre.*

# DOG KENNEL WALK (OR PATH)

An ancient right of way originally leading to Houghton Hall. I have been told there were hunt kennels at the Hall. Certainly the Dunstable Gazette recalls that the North Herts Hunt met at the Hall in 1935. Mr Fred Moore recalls the Hunt Kennels kept at the Hall by Colonel Part which in the 1920's were hare hounds or harriers and Colonel Part was the Master.

*Dog Kennel Walk between Dunstable Grammar School (now Ashton Middle School) and Grove House Gardens looking towards the railway footbridge in the early 1930's.*

# DORCHESTER CLOSE

Mrs Margaret Lines, who conducted a detailed study of street names for Dunstable Museum Trust, was told that this relates to the famous London Hotel. The connection with Dunstable is, however, unclear.

*An aerial view of Kingscroft Avenue and Dorchester Close in September 1966. The market is in full swing on the Queensway Hall Car Park but other car parks in the town centre are comparatively free of cars. In the top left hand corner, in High Street North, the demolition of the former Town Hall is nearly complete and in the centre left can be seen the Dunstable Town Bowling Green. (DG)*

# FRIARS WALK AND FRIARY FIELD

These are respectively adjacent to and partly on the site of the Dominican Friary of St Mary's which was founded in 1259 and stood on the opposite side of High Street from the Augustinian Priory of St Peter. The Manshead Archaeological Society undertook a series of digs on the site of the Friary and uncovered a wealth of interesting material. The most significant find was the Swan Jewel found in 1965 (see Swan Court).

*Excavated ovens of the Dominican Friary in about 1965. (MAS)*

*The putting green of Mr Costin in Friary Field in the early 1970's. (MAS)*

*A BBC film crew from the programme "Chronicle" film the Manshead Archaeological Society's excavations in 1979. (MAS)*

*The entrance to Friary Field in 1985. (BCC)*

# ICKNIELD STREET

Refers to the pre-historic Icknield Way which followed the escarpment of the Chiltern Hills from the Ridgeway to Peddars Way in Norfolk.

*Dunstable's first Police Station built in 1867 at the junction of Burr Street and Icknield Street photographed in 1963. (DG)*

# ICKNIELD VILLAS

Developed around a 19th century mansion of the same name which was once owned by the Tibbett family who started the Index Printing works.

*The original Icknield Villa in 1876 showing members of the Tibbett family, the original owners (see Index Court and Tibbett Close).(PB)*

# KINGSWAY

Originally laid out as a residential cul-de-sac in 1935, both the name of the road and that of the Developers, Kingscroft Estates, refer to the Royal Palace or Hunting Lodge of Kingsbury which stood on the site of the present Norman King, the Old Palace Lodge Hotel and Kingsbury Court.

*A queue for potato rationing during the First World War at Kingsbury Farm House in Church Street in April 1917. This site is now the entrance to Kingsway.*

*A rural scene on the site of what is now Kingsway and Bernard Close showing in the background Ladies Lodge Almshouses (on the left) and the Priory Church (on the right) taken by Luton News Photographer R G Cooper in August 1938. (LM/DG)*

BEDFORDSHIRE COUNTY COUNCIL EDUCATION COMMITTEE

*College of Further Education*

**KINGSWAY · DUNSTABLE**

PROSPECTUS

1

SESSION 1961-2

*The first prospectus for the newly opened Dunstable College in Kingsway in 1961.*

*Kingsway looking north from the junction with Bernard Close in 1985. (BCC)*

*Kingsbury riding stables (now the Norman King Public House) in Kingsway at its junction with Church Street in 1936. (LM/DG)*

# KINGSBURY COURT

This modern housing development takes the name of Kingsbury House which has been incorporated as part of the development. Originally built in about 1120 several medieval kings held court here. The building was later placed under the responsibility of the Priory and after the dissolution of the Monasteries it became a farm in 1542. The present buildings were likely constructed in the 18th century, probably re-using earlier stone either from the Priory or the original Palace. For much of the 20th century the House was the home of Dr Gerald and Mrs Mary Ashton, who both played a full and active part in town life and who on their death expressed a wish that the property be developed for use by older people. The Ashtons are remembered in the name of Ashton House, the headquarters of the Manshead Archaeological Society in Winfield Street whose purchase they supported.

*The home and surgery of Dr Gerald Ashton in about 1950. (DG)*

*The modern housing development in the grounds of Kingsbury Court in 1990. (AW)*

# KINGSCROFT AVENUE

Named after the development company, Kingscroft Estates, started by Mr T W Flory and continued by his son, Clifford Flory. The company was responsible for much inter - war development in Dunstable.

# THE MALL

When this new development was proposed in the mid 1970's the Councillors were asked to select a name on a regal theme to match the nearby Kingsway and Queensway. I have been told that one felt the suggestions were rather pretentious and facetiously suggested the Council should go the whole hog and call the road "The Mall". His colleagues, however, liked the name and adopted it. The developers have since given the blocks of flats individual names of Princes Court, Dukes Court, Duchess Court, Earls Court, Kings Court and Queens Court whilst retaining the original consecutive numbers. This is most confusing as Queens Court already exists, albeit with different numbers, in High Street North.

*Stephen and Janice Fountain win £100 as the first purchasers of a flat at The Mall in December 1977. (DG)*

# MIDDLE ROW

Originally called "Middle Rents" these buildings between High Street South and Ashton Square originated as market stalls in the middle of the main road, the covers of which became permanent in the 14th century.

*The 1919 Peace Celebrations pass Middle Row.(LM/DG)*

*An aerial view of the Dunstable Crossroads in 1974 showing in the bottom centre the properties of Middle Row. In the lower right the construction of the Priory Health Centre has just started. (Aerofilms)*

# NICHOLAS WAY

Part of the Quadrant Shopping Centre recalls Nicholas Lane which used to lead from High Street North to the premises of Dunstable Town Bowls Club.

*Sorting herbs for Flemons and Marchant, probably in Nicholas Lane. The young lad wearing a cap is Mr Frank Hutchins. (DG)*

*Nicholas Way in 1976. (AM)*

*The entrance to Nicholas Way from High Street South in 1985. (BCC)*

## NORTON COURT

Constructed on the site of Stuart & Sons hat factory (one of the last to operate in Dunstable) this recent flats development retains the name of Norton House on its High Street frontage. This fine Georgian building was once the home of the factory manager.

## QUADRANT

The A5 (Watling Street) and the A505 (Icknield Way) effectively divide Dunstable into four "quadrants". The commercial and civic redevelopment of the north - east quadrant in the early 1960's was a significant achievement for the time. The pedestrianised shopping precinct opened by Bob Monkhouse on 3rd June 1966 was named simply "The Quadrant".

*Members of the Manshead Archaeological Society excavating the site of a Roman Road as The Quadrant Shopping Centre development takes place in 1964. The current Chairman of the Society, Mrs Joan Schneider, can be seen in the checked shirt. (MAS)*

*The Quadrant Shopping Centre and its distinctive clock in 1986. (Alan Hill)*

# QUEENSWAY

The short section of shopping street connecting High Street with Court Drive and nearby Civic Hall was named as a companion for Kingsway. The name "Queensway Hall" was originally proposed for the main hall only of the Civic Centre but the Council later adopted the name for the whole building to coincide with the 10th anniversary of the Coronation of Queen Elizabeth II.

*The Queensway Hall under construction in 1963. Queensway itself has only just been completed as a highway in the top left hand corner. (DG)*

*Sir James Harman, Lord Mayor of London, opens the Queensway Hall on 16th April 1964 watched by the Mayor, Alderman Michael Kilby, and a large crowd of interested Dunstablians. (DG)*

*The completed Queensway Hall in 1964.*

*Queensway in February 1964 showing on the right the former fire station shortly before its move to the junction of High Street North and Brewers Hill Road. (BT)*

*The same view as in the previous picture but taken from The Union Bingo Club with the fire station site now a temporary car park in July 1975. (BT)*

*Queensway looking towards the Hall in 1996. (SBDC)*

# ST MARY'S GATE

The main access to the Wilkinson's car park retains the name of St Mary's Street which originally ran parallel to West Street and was once called Pothyn Lane. The Dominican Friary which stood nearby in High Street South (see Friary Field) was dedicated to St Mary.

*Members of the Manshead Archaeological Society excavating the site of what was to become the Divisional Police Headquarters at the corner of St Mary's Gate and West Street in 1974.(MAS)*

# SCOTT COURT

Alderman Benjamin James Scott, the proprietor of Scott's Garage in High Street South, was Mayor from 1952-54. His daughter Miss Christina Scott JP was headmistress of Queen Eleanor's and Queensbury Schools. The Coronation Medal presented to Alderman Scott when he attended the Coronation of Elizabeth II is on display at Grove House.

*Scott's Garage in High Street South in the 1930's.*

*Alderman Ben Scott (centre in Mayoral Robes) at the consecration of the extension to Dunstable Cemetery 17th June 1952. (DG)*

*Alderman Scott accompanies Miss Joan Gilbert, a TV announcer, and the Mayor and Mayoress of Bedford at the 1952 Carnival on the lawns of Grove House. (DG)*

# THE LAWNS

The footpath linking High Street North with Vernon Place is named after the large house which once stood next to Grove House and on part of whose site it is situated.

*The Coronation Carnival in High Street North showing the large garden of The Lawns next to Grove House . (BT)*

*The Lawns (obscured by the large trees) and the adjoining building in High Street North being demolished in May 1959 to make way for the construction of Queensway and the development that now includes Argos and Iceland. (BT)*

*The Lawns in spring 1999.*

## VERNON PLACE

James Vernon was the Director of Waterlows responsible for bringing the company to Dunstable where he later served as residential manager until 1901 when he was succeeded by his son, James William Vernon.

*Vernon Place in 1976 showing the Library and Queensway Hall taken from the temporary car park in Queensway vacated by the relocation of the fire station and prior to the construction of Queensway Parade (the row of shops which now includes Peacocks). (BCC)*

*Dunstable market at the second of its recent homes on the Queensway Hall car park taken from the office development in Vernon Place in February 1977. 76 stalls could be accommodated on this site compared with the 30 possible in High Street North prior to the move in 1963. Subsequent moves to the north of the Queensway Hall and now to The Square and Ashton Square allow for an even larger number of stalls. (BT)*

*A montage of Vernon Place in 1995 showing Dunstable Library undergoing roof repairs.*

## WOOD STREET

A small passageway south of the Saracens Head is all that remains of an ancient right of way from Houghton Regis to Buckwood or (Beechwood) near Markyate.

# Chapter 2 - WEST CENTRAL

With the exception of limited development east of the Priory Church, most of the initial expansion of Dunstable during the 19th Century took place to the west of the town centre. The British Land Company bought large tracts of land in this area and was responsible for the initial laying out of many of the streets. The standard of construction was, however, poor and it was often many years later before the road surfaces were made up to a standard acceptable to the Council for adoption as publicly maintained highways.

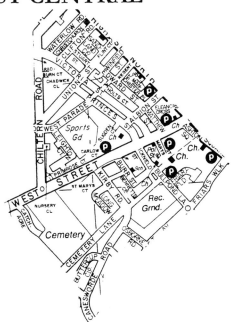

## ALBION STREET

Previously Albion Road. Developed by the British Land Company from 1861 onwards. "Albion" is Latin for "Britain".

*Barry Horne, Secretary of the Manshead Archaeological Society, inspects the Society's excavations on the site of the future Eleanors Court development in Albion Street in 1981. The Society discovered a well and a Roman burial site as well as the foundations of early cottages. (JS)*

*Two views of Albion Street looking west in 1995.*

# BEALE STREET

The Beal (sic) family owned a flour mill in this street which was taken over by Marshall's Whiting Works and Stonemasons in 1853. Many memorials made by Marshall's can be seen in the older part of the Cemetery in West Street.

**ALFRED MARSHALL**
LATE THOMAS MARSHALL.
**MONUMENTAL MASON,**
BEALE STREET, DUNSTABLE.
TAKES this opportunity of announcing that he has succeeded to the Business carried on for so many years in Dunstable by his late Father, and hopes to merit a continuance of the same Patronage and Support, by the prompt execution in a superior style of all orders entrusted to his care, at the lowest possible prices.
MONUMENTS, TOMBS,
HEADSTONES IN GRANITE,
MARBLE OR STONE, Neatly Executed.

*An advertisement for Marshall's Stone Masons in February 1885.*

*Beale Street in 1999.*

# BENNETTS CLOSE

The Bennett Family owned the town's principal brewery which stood at the junction of Chiltern Road and High Street North now occupied by the Priory Roast Inn. Benjamin Bennett the younger was Mayor in 1871-2 and his grandson left to the town the land which now forms Bennett Memorial Recreation Ground. Bennett's beer and ginger ale bottles, once commonplace items, are now eagerly collected.

*Benjamin Bennett in 1871.*

*Bennetts Close shortly after the completion of older persons' bungalows in August 1962. (BT)*

# BUNKERS COURT

Built on the site of Mr Robert Bunker's butchers shop. Bunker's sausages were a renowned local delicacy.

# BURR STREET

Originally owned by Thomas Burr, an important Brewer who owned several inns. The present road was developed by his nephew Edward Burr, initially in two parts. The section off Bull Pond Lane/Icknield Street was known as Burr Street and the West Street section was known as "Upper Burr Street" until 1920 when the two roads were joined. Burr's Brewery stood on the site now occupied by the Union Bingo Club in High Street North.

*Dolman Bros, Hat and Bonnet block makers, Burr Street in about 1930. (MD)*

*Icknield Lower School,*
*previously Burr Street*
*School in 1986. (BCC)*

TO THE MEMORY
OF
THOMAS BURR ESQ.
LATE OF THIS PARISH
THIS TABLET
IS
AFFECTIONATELY DEDICATED
HE WAS BORN AUGUST 2 1778
HE DEPARTED THIS LIFE JULY 13
AND HIS REMAINS WERE DEPOSITED
IN THE FAMILY VAULT AT LUTON JULY 21
1835.

*The Burr Memorial in the*
*Priory Church.*

# BUTTERCUP CLOSE

Part of the original Croft Estate. Buttercup Lane was the original name for Canesworde Road and is retained today by the section which leads from the Canesworde Road/Meadway junction to the Golf Course past Ardley Heights Scout HQ. Alternative names initially considered by the Council in 1956 were "Canesworde Close" and "Downs View Close".

# CANESWORDE ROAD

The oldest part of this road follows the route of an ancient trackway (originally known as Buttercup Lane) to Kensworth, spelt "Canesworde" in the Doomsday Book. Part of the original route, leading beyond Hurlock Close across the Golf Course, is still called Buttercup Lane today.

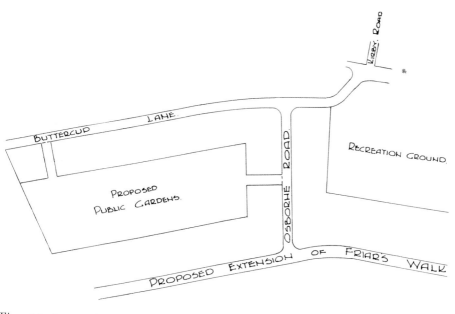

*The original estate plan for the Croft Estate in 1936 showing Canesworde Road still referred to by its original name "Buttercup Lane".*

*A 1955 advertisement for new houses in Canesworde Road.*

# CATCHACRE

The ancient field name for this site off West Street. The Council originally acquired the site for allotments in 1921 and part was sold for housing in 1989 to fund a Cemetery extension and the construction of the Downside Community Centre among other projects. The field appears to have straddled the original boundaries between Dunstable and Kensworth and was subject to an ownership dispute between Dunstable Priory and the Parish of Kensworth which may in some way have given rise to this name.

*An extract from the 1989 brochure for the sale of part of Catchacre Allotments for housing.*

# CEMETERY LANE

A long-established right of way leading from Spoondell Quarry to Whiting Works at the junction of Icknield Street and Bull Pond Lane. The lane now runs at the rear of Dunstable Cemetery which was opened in 1861 when burials ceased in the Priory Churchyard. It has since been extended into the adjoining allotments on several occasions.

*The Chapels at Dunstable Cemetery viewed from the Cemetery Lane entrance in 1998*

# CHADWICK CLOSE

Built on the site of the former Council Highways and Sewers Depot, Edwin Chadwick was the famous Victorian Public Health Reformer .

*The entrance to the former Council Depot in Union Street (now Chadwick Court) in December 1993. (DB)*

# CHILTERN COURT

This comparatively new development in Chiltern Road is built on the site of Bourn's Whiting Works, once an important Dunstable industry. The proposal to so name it was referred back to the Highways Committee by the full Town Council in 1969 and it was initially agreed to name it "Derbyshire Court" after the former Mayor and local author, W H Derbyshire. The suggestion was unpopular and the original proposal prevailed.

*W H Derbyshire*

*Signed title page of Derbyshire's History of Dunstable, published in expanded form in 1872*

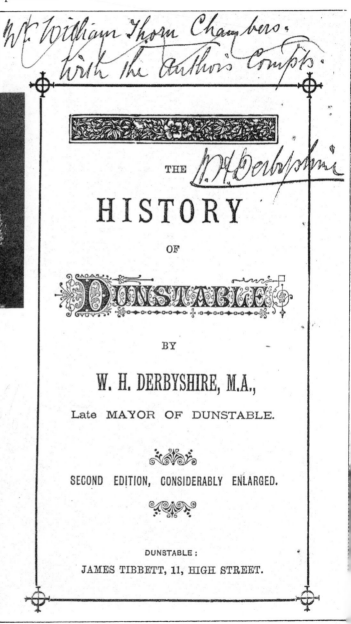

THE

HISTORY

OF

Dunstable

BY

W. H. DERBYSHIRE, M.A.,

Late MAYOR OF DUNSTABLE.

SECOND EDITION, CONSIDERABLY ENLARGED.

DUNSTABLE:
JAMES TIBBETT, 11, HIGH STREET.

# CHILTERN ROAD

Refers to the Chiltern Hills and was originally built sometime before 1866 between Union Street and High Street North. The length from Union Street towards Dunstable Cemetery in West Street was an unmade track originally known locally as "Cemetery Road". The roundabout at the junction with West Street was completed in 1974.

*Chiltern Road about 1920. (BS)*

*A similar view in 1999.*

111

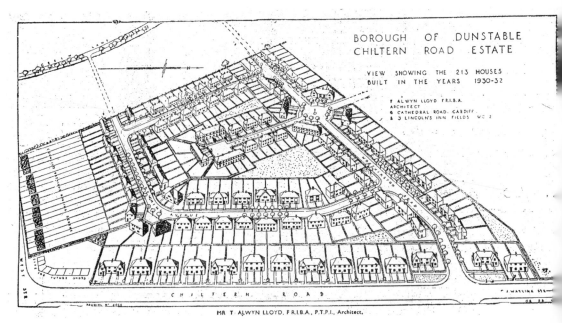

*The architect, T Alwyn Lloyd's sketch of the Chiltern Road housing development, completed between 1930-32*

| | 1st Section (120 hses) | | 2nd Section (93 hses) | | Whole Scheme (213 hses) | |
|---|---|---|---|---|---|---|
| | Total Cost | Average Per House | Total Cost | Average Per House | Total Cost | Average Per House |
| Site | 984 13 4 | 8 4 8 | 683 14 2 | 7 7 | 1641 4 9 | 4 16 |
| Roads | 4251 2 6 | 35 8 6 | 2314 2 10 | 24 17 8 | 6565 5 4 | 30 16 |
| Sewers | 1405 3 11 | 11 14 2 | 949 . 5 | 10 4 1 | 2354 4 4 | 11 1 |
| Buildings | 50163 13 11 | 418 - 8 | 34358 8 4 | 369 8 | 84522 2 6 | 396 16 |
| | 56804 13 11 | 473 8 - | 38305 6 . | 411 14 8 | 95112 19 11 | 446 10 |

*An extract from a 1934 Council report showing the final accounts for the Chiltern Road scheme, indicating that each house cost £396 on average to build.*

# CLIFTON ROAD

Originally part of the Bull Close Estate, the Bull Inn still stands on High Street North. Whilst other roads in the estate have names of obvious significance to Dunstable, the choice of Clifton was not immediately apparent. However, Mr James Vernon, the Waterlow's Director responsible for bringing the company to Dunstable, lived in Clifton Road, Kilburn in London. The principal demand for houses came from Waterlow's employees, which is why the neighbouring street is named after the company, so it is reasonable to assume that Mr Vernon influenced this street being named after his own home address. The road was laid out in 1908 and was the first street in all of the roads off High Street North to be tree-lined.

*Small's timber yard in Clifton Road in June 1993. (DB)*

*The same view in 1995 showing new houses built on the site. (DB)*

# CROSS STREET NORTH

A link road between Beale Street and Chiltern Road. There was previously a Cross Street West which linked St Mary's Street and West Street broadly along the line of the present St Mary Gate.

*Cross Street North in April 1999.*

# EDWARD STREET

Most roads in this locality have a royal or patriotic origin and it could be that this refers to one of Queen Victoria's eldest sons, Prince Edward, the Prince of Wales. An alternative is that it refers to Edward Burr (see Burr Street) who once owned the land. The section between Regent Street and Union Street was shown as "Mount Street" in the 1851 census and in the 1861 town Directory but it had disappeared by the time of the 1876 Directory (see map under "Winfield Street").

*A postcard about 1910 showing Kilby's bakery in Edward Street. The bakery, now known as Creamer's, remains popular today. (BS)*

*The Borough Arms coach outing assembles in Edward Street in June 1967. (BT)*

*Cottages and Hat Factory at the junction of Edward Street and Regent Street being demolished in April 1962. (BT)*

*New maisonettes on the same site as the last picture in February 1977. (BT)*

*Edward Street in November 1978. (DG)*

# ELEANOR'S CROSS

This modern shopping precinct takes its name from one of the 13 crosses erected in 1291 by Edward I to mark the overnight resting places of the Funeral Cortege of his Queen Eleanor of Castile. The Dunstable Cross stood near the crossroads and an explanatory plaque is located on the wall of National Westminster Bank. A fine statue of Queen Eleanor by Dora Barrett and commissioned by the developers, Robinson and White,now has pride of place in the shopping precinct. The events of 1291 were also remembered in the naming of Queen Eleanor's Grammar School for girls in Langdale Road which now forms part of Queensbury School.

*The unveiling ceremony for the statue of Queen Eleanor in the Eleanor's Cross precinct in September 1985 showing, Mr Colin White (developer), Dora Barrett, the sculptress and Councillor and Mrs Bob Cook, the Chairman of South Bedfordshire District Council. (BCC)*

# FLINT COURT

Built opposite the site of Flinte House, a distinctive 19th century property with flint fascia on the walls.

*Flinte House in High Street North in 1975 (BC)*

# HOLTS COURT

George Holt (affectionately known as Dobbin Holt) was a Councillor and Alderman for the former South Ward from 1926-45. He lived at Dell House in Church Street.

*An affectionate cartoon of "Dobbin" Holt included in the 1931 "Dunstable Book" published to celebrate the 25th Anniversary of the founding of Dunstable Downs Golf Club.*

MR. DOBBIN HOLT, THE EMINENT BEDFORDSHIRE POET

# KIRBY ROAD

Laid out in 1880 on the site of a field originally known as "Kirby Close".

# LEIGHTON COURT

This 1968 development retains the name of the ancient footpath which links it with West Street, known for centuries as "Leighton Gap".

# LONG MEADOW

A traditional field name which once formed part of Headey's market gardening business. The present development was completed in September 1984.

# MANCHESTER PLACE

A small terrace of former Victorian artisans' dwellings which were demolished in 1959 to make way for the Pioneer Boys Club and Dunstable Young People's Club, which were funded by a Mayoral appeal. It has been suggested that it was originally built to accommodate workers from Stuart and Sons hat factory which relocated from Manchester and which stood on the site of the Union Bingo Club. When the factory closed in 1920 the building was used as temporary residential accommodation and was colloquially known as "The Manor House" until it was closed in 1933 as being unfit for habitation. This has confused several recent commentators as the real Dunstable Manor House stood a few yards further along High Street North on the site of the Old Post Office.

*The junction of Manchester Place and High Street North in May 1973 showing the Conservative Club before it was extended. (BT)*

# MAYOR OF DUNSTABLE'S
# £5,000 APPEAL

DINNER

HALFWAY HOUSE HOTEL, DUNSTABLE

MONDAY, JUNE 1st, 1959

## MENU

CREAM OF ASPARAGUS

SILVER HAKE WITH SHRIMP SAUCE

ABERDEEN ANGUS RUMP STEAK
WITH MUSHROOMS

NEW AND CHIPPED POTATOES

RUNNER BEANS

ICED GATEAU

COFFEE

*The menu card for a Civic Dinner in June 1959 to launch the Appeal for the construction of the Pioneer Boys and Dunstable Young People's Clubs in Manchester Place.*

# MATTHEW STREET

Matthew Gutteridge, a farmer and landowner, sold the land on which this street was developed in 1865. The section nearest to Albion Street was originally known as "Mount Street".

*Matthew Street in 1995.*

# MAYPOLE YARD

Access between numbers 14 and 16 West Street, potentially an attractive courtyard, Worthington Smith in his history of Dunstable suggests that traditional dancing around the maypole actually took place here in the mid 19th century.

*Maypole Yard in February 1970 before the renovation of several of the buildings. (DB)*

# NURSERY CLOSE

Built on the site of the Cottage Garden Nurseries owned by three generations of the Headey Family.

*The Cottage Garden Nursery in Chiltern Road in October 1993 shortly before its demolition. (DB)*

*The completed redevelopment in July 1995. (DB)*

# OSBORNE ROAD

Joseph Osborn, a Maltster of West Street was Mayor in 1865-7 and whose name appears above the first Police Station (see illustration under Icknield Street), but the road is more likely to relate to "Osborne Close" an original field name in this locality.

*Osborne Road in 1999. (PH)*

*Joseph Osborn in 1866*

# PRIMROSE COURT

This modern development, built in 1970, retains the name of the Primrose Laundry which stood on the site until its closure in 1969. The adjacent houses on West Street still display the name "Primrose Cottages". The Council suggested it should be named Derbyshire Court after the former Mayor and distinguished local historian WH Derbyshire. The developer was, however, adamant and responded that he "did not see why private estates should be named after deceased citizens".

This is, in fact, the third occasion I have come across when a street was unsuccessfully proposed to be named in memory of Mr Derbyshire - a situation which will perhaps be remedied one day.

# PRINCES STREET

Constructed sometime before 1871 this road follows a common "Royal" theme with others in the area and probably refers to the sons of Queen Victoria.

*An aerial view of St Mary's Church in July 1972 showing, from right to left, Princes, Victoria and Matthew streets. (Aerofilms)*

*Princes Street in November 1978. (LM/DG)*

*Princes Street in November 1995. (SBDC)*

## RADBURN COURT

Built by Robinson and White in, at the time, a new American type of layout where pedestrian and vehicular access are physically separate, which originated in Radburn, New Jersey.

## REGENT STREET

Continuing the Royal theme of roads in this area and probably referring to the Prince Regent, later King George IV.

*Regent Street in November 1978. (DG)*

# SANDLAND CLOSE

This maisonette development is named after the late Tommy Sandland who was a Council Member from 1938-55 and Mayor from 1949-52. He officiated at both the opening of Dunstable Cricket Ground in Bull Pond Lane and the dedication of the town's War Memorial in Priory Gardens.

*Thomas Sandland in Mayoral Robes in 1949.*

*The Mayor, Tommy Sandland, presiding at the dedication of the Dunstable War Memorial in Priory Gardens in May 1952. (LM/DG)*

# STEWART CLARK COURT

Mr E Stewart Clark was Chairman of South Bedfordshire District Council and the first Town Mayor of Dunstable following the dissolution of the Borough Council in March 1974.

*E Stewart Clark in Mayoral Robes*

# STUART STREET

Could refer to the Royal Household as other roads in this vicinity have a regal connection. A more likely suggestion is a reference to Stuart & Sons, the last hat manufacturers to operate in Dunstable.

*Stuart Street Coronation Street Party in June 1953. (BT)*

# SUGDEN COURT

The Aldwyck Housing Association were responsible for this development which is named after their Director, Mr G A Sugden, who sadly died before its completion in 1977.

# SWAN COURT

Commemorates the famous discovery of the Swan Jewel at the nearby Dominican Friary (now Friary Field) in 1965. The gold and enamel brooch is now on display in the British Museum. The present development was built by Robinson and White in 1985 on the site of a branch of Cogswell's Whiting Works.

*The Swan Jewel at its point of discovery in Friary Field in 1965. (MAS)*

*Cogswell's Whiting Works seen from Bennett Memorial Recreation Ground in 1939.*

# UNION STREET

One suggestion is that this is a Royal name commemorating the Union of England, Scotland, Wales and Ireland. More likely it refers to the former Dunstable Poor Law Union as it formed the northern boundary of the Dunstable Parish at the time. Poor Law administration was amalgamated with Luton in 1835 and the Dunstable Workhouse in High Street South (near the White Swan Inn) was closed.

*An aerial view, about 1920, of the High Street North area showing in the foreground, Union Street, Winfield Street and Regent Street. In the background is the Waterlow's Printing Works but in the top left hand corner, the road to Houghton Regis (Mixt Way) is still a small country lane with no cement works. (LM/DG)*

*An aerial view looking east from the Chiltern Road/Union Street junction in the late 1930's with the "new" Drill Hall in Victoria Street in the centre of the picture. In the top the cement works in Houghton Regis is now fully operational but Douglas Crescent has yet to be completed. (DG)*

# THE MALTINGS

Built on the site of former maltings associated with Bennett's Brewery.

*The Maltings under construction in about 1992. (SBDC)*

# VICTORIA STREET

Queen Victoria who reigned from 1837 to 1901 was the last reigning Monarch to visit Dunstable when she and Prince Albert visited the Sugar Loaf Hotel in 1841.

*The opening of the Victoria Street Congregational Church after alterations in September 1957. (BT)*

*Victoria Street in November 1978. (DG)*

*The nostalgic window display of Berry's Off-licence in Victoria Street in March 1961. (BT)*

# WATERLOW ROAD

Part of the town developed by the British Land Company to accommodate print workers who moved with Waterlow and Sons from London in 1891. By 1960 the company were employing 1200 people but only a fraction of this number are now employed on the replacement factory in Foster Avenue. The original works are now a housing development known as Printers Way.

*Smalls Timber Yard in Waterlow Road in September 1993. (DB)*

*New homes on the same site in July 1995. (DB)*

# WEST PARADE

Laid out by the Council in 1896 the first parade of 15 houses was built between 1900 and 1909 and formed the then western boundary of the town.

*West Parade in about 1910 from an old postcard.*

*Dunstable Grammar School playing field in West Parade in the shadow of the West Street Windmill in about 1900.*

# WINFIELD STREET

The late 19th century ordnance survey maps show a Winfield iron works in this area.

*Winfield Street showing the former Sportsman Pub (now the Les Matthews Archaeology Centre) in June 1962. (BT)*

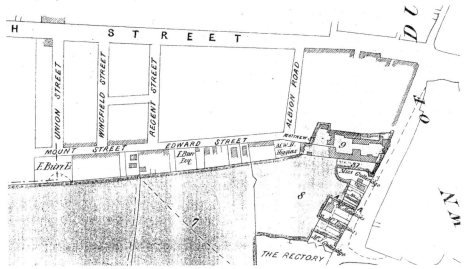

*An extract from the Abstract of Title of the British Land Company in 1861 showing Winfield Street spelt with a "g" and also showing Mount Street (see Edward Street).*

# Chapter 3 - PRIORY WARD

The area bounded by Church Street and High Street South/London Road comprises the Priory electoral ward. The area has been developed in three distinct phases. Firstly the Englands Close and Borough Farm Estates together with the streets near the Great Northern railway station were laid out between 1890 and the First World War. These were followed by several comparatively small scale developments by a variety of private builders in the Half Moon Lane area. The southern section was developed as the Downside Council housing Estate from the early 1950's.

*An aerial view of the Downside Estate in the late 1950's. To the left of the picture the Mayfield Road shopping parade had yet to be built as had Jardine Way which now occupies the empty field in the centre of the photograph beneath Blows Down. In the foreground is the Stipers Hill Estate (see chapter 9) which has not yet been extended by the addition of Burges Close and Birchside.(DG)*

# ALBERT COURT

Previously Albert Street.  Named after Prince Albert, Consort to Queen Victoria.

*Albert Street off High Street South in 1957. (BT)*

*The old people's flats development now known as Albert Court which replaced Albert Street in February 1977. (BT)*

# ALFRED STREET

First laid out in 1882 as part of the Englands Close Estate although the houses were actually built some years later by Alfred Bandy after whom the street is named.

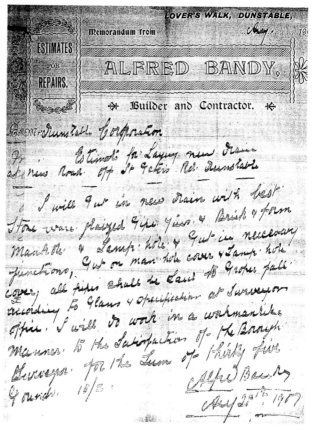

*Mr Alfred Bandy presents his estimate to the Council in August 1907 for laying sewers in his "new road off St Peter's Road" for the sum of £35.10s*

*Alfred Street in 1999. (BS)*

# ALLEN CLOSE

Bill Allen was three times Mayor of Dunstable in 1967/68, 1980/81 and 1984/85. A Plant Supervisor at Electrolux in Luton, he is mainly remembered for his long service with the scouting movement and for nine years was Chairman of the District Scout Association.

*Alderman Bill Allen in 1967.*

*Allen Close in 1999. (BS)*

## APOLLO CLOSE

Together with Chichester Close was built on the site of the Downside Estate development of post-war prefabricated houses. Commemorates the first moon landing of Apollo 11 in July 1969. The residents of the original prefabs were re-housed in new council housing to the south of the town which retained the original estate name "Downside". This road also has the unusual distinction of having two street name plates each with a different spelling, "Apollo" and "Appollo".

*Immediately after the Second World War there was a crisis of insufficient housing accommodation in Dunstable and many other towns which led to this general appeal for emergency accommodation in 1945. A further response to the problem was the construction of the Downside pre-fabricated housing scheme in 1946 on what is today Apollo Close and Chichester Close.*

# BARTON AVENUE

Built in 1936, believed to be named after the Barton Family, who were farmers and provision merchants. Richard Barton, who was Mayor of Dunstable in 1883/85, lived at the property in Great Northern Road now known as "The Grange" and it is believed that his landholding included the site of this road. His brother Frederick was closely associated with the building of Waterlow Road Methodist Church. This family are also related to the Hollywood film star, Gary Cooper, who was educated at Dunstable Grammar School. The road was made up in 1956 at a cost of £2,049 and subsequently adopted by the Council.

*Councillor Richard Barton in his Mayoral Robes.*

*Flooding in Barton Avenue in 1955 whilst it was still a privately-maintained street.*

# BIGTHAN ROAD

The road's development coincided with the move to Dunstable in 1909 of Cross Paperware, whose premises were originally known as "The Bigthan Works". Bigthan apparently comes from the ancient Persian meaning of "gift of God" and is referred to in the Book of Esther. The firm's original owners, Henry Cross and Frederick Escott were both devout men and it is likely that they purposefully selected the name.

---

## "BIGTHAN WORKS," DUNSTABLE
*The largest Lace Paper Factory in the World*

## The Home of the world-famous brand of "CROSSCO"
## TABLE STATIONERY OF DISTINCTION

*Manufactured by British Workpeople and from British Material the "CROSSCO" brand stands supreme in its class*

# CROSS AND COMPANY LIMITED
SPECIALISTS IN ALL GRADES OF

| | |
|---|---|
| LACE PAPER D'OYLEYS | CRIMPED PAPER CASES |
| EMBOSSED DISH & PLATE PAPERS | FRILLS |
| TRAY PAPERS | PULP PICNIC REQUISITES |
| SERVIETTES | SOUFFLE CASES |

AND EVERY DESCRIPTION OF ARTICLES FOR TABLE DECORATION & SERVICE OF FOOD

---

*A 1936 advertisement for the Bigthan Works of Cross Paperware.*

*Bigthan Road in 1999. (BS)*

| Item | Description | Detail | £ | s | d |
|---|---|---|---|---|---|
|  | Manual labour |  | 24 |  | 11 |
|  | Rollings |  |  | 7 |  |
|  | Costin (contract) |  | 9 | 10 | 10 |
|  | do " |  | 4 |  | 6 |
| Rubble | Corporation of Dunstable | 79 loads brick rubble | 3 | 19 |  |
| Clinkers | " " | 11 " clinkers |  | 11 |  |
|  | Gas Company " | 9 " " |  | 9 |  |
|  | Robinson Jas. | 48 " brick rubble | 2 | 8 |  |
|  | Lester | 24 " " | 1 | 4 |  |
|  | Headly | 3 " " |  | 3 |  |
|  | Phipps & Co. |  | 20 | 2 |  |
|  | do |  | 9 | 15 | 6 |
|  | do |  | 2 | 10 |  |
|  | do |  | 3 | 17 | 1 |
| Shingles | Butterfield |  | 2 | 10 |  |
| Cement | Forders |  | 2 | 5 | 6 |
|  | do |  |  | 10 | 10 |
|  | do |  |  | 5 |  |
| opening tools | Mead |  |  | 10 |  |
| Wharf Rent | Gt Northern Railway Co. |  | 5 | 5 |  |
| steam rolling | Powdrill G. |  | 27 | 14 |  |
| Patent Stove | Excelsior Stove Co. |  | 2 | 5 |  |
| Iron work | Boro' Engineering Works |  | 1 | 3 |  |
| do | do |  | 44 |  | 7 |
| Timber & gullies | Brown H. & Sons |  | 3 | 14 |  |
| Tar | Luton Gas Co. |  |  | 11 | 6 |
| Printing | Waterlow & Sons. |  | 3 | 15 |  |
| Clerk of works | Stewart J |  | 1 | 17 | 3 |
| Allowance for path | Jemms J H. |  | 2 | 10 |  |
| Lighting | Dunstable Gas Co |  | 2 | 10 | 9 |
| Sols Costs | Benning & Son |  | 1 | 1 |  |
| Iypt. | Taylor Geo. |  | £145 | 6 | 3 |

*The final account for making up Bigthan Road as a publicly maintained highway in 1909.*

143

## BLOWS ROAD

Leads to Blows Downs named after John Blow, a former proprietor of Poynters Farm (see Poynters Road) whose land originally included the Downs.

*Blows Downs in January 1939.(LM/DG)*

## BRITAIN STREET

A typical Victorian patriotic street naming and logical for a road once forming part of Englands Lane.

*Two views of Britain Street in 1999. (BS)*

# BOROUGH ROAD

Originally ran parallel to the Borough boundary and formed part of the Borough Farm Estate which was laid out after 1895 between Great Northern Road and Half Moon Lane. Many of the original farm buildings are still in existence.

*An advertisement for the sale of building plots in Borough Road and other parts of the Borough Farm Estate in 1895. Keen-eyed readers will note that the original proprietors, Messrs Garside, were offering "wine on the table at 6.45 sharp"!*

# BRIVE ROAD

Originally called Beechwood Avenue in view of the large row of beech trees which were to have lined the centre of the road. However, the plans did not materialise and only those trees remaining on the green in Mayfield Road have survived from the original hedge line. The road was renamed in 1956 (to avoid confusion with Buckwood Avenue) after Dunstable's French Twin Town Brive-la-Gaillarde.

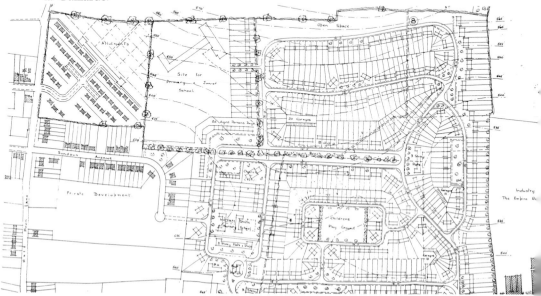

*The original plan for the Downside Estate in August 1951 showing in the centre the initial proposal for a wide avenue (later Brive Road) to be built around a line of existing beech trees. On the left of the plan can be seen the original layout of the first "Downside" estate of pre-fabricated houses which was subsequently redeveloped as Apollo Close and Chichester Close. Sundown Avenue is also shown as a cul-de-sac leading from Half Moon Lane*

*Brive Road looking towards Oakwood Avenue in March 1961. (BT)*

*The late Mr Allan Townsend, a street lighting engineer, repairing a column near his own home in Brive Road in about 1965. (MT)*

*Brive Road looking towards the flats in Southwood Road in 1976. (AM)*

## CHICHESTER CLOSE

Built on the site of the Half Moon Lane war time pre-fabs known as "The Downside Estate". The current name commemorates Sir Francis Chichester who sailed single-handed around the World in Gypsy Moth IV in 1966/67 just prior to the start of this development.

## DOWNS ROAD

A suitable name for a road leading towards Blows Downs.

*Downs Road in June 1999.(BS)*

## DRAKES COURT

Originally proposed as "Grange Court" after the large house behind which these flats were built. The Town Council's alternative suggestion was accepted as the development coincided with the major local celebrations in 1988 to commemorate the 400th anniversary of the defeat of the Spanish Armada by Sir Francis Drake.

*Drakes Court in April 1999.*

## ELIZABETH COURT

This new housing development in England's Lane was named in honour of our present Monarch whose 60th Birthday coincided with the completion of the houses in 1986.

# BOROUGH OF DUNSTABLE

The Proclamation of the Accession of Her Majesty Queen Elizabeth II. will be read from the Town Hall tomorrow Friday 8th February, 1952, at 2-30 p.m.

*Thomas Sandland.*
**Mayor.**

**Mayor's Parlour,
    Dunstable.
7th February, 1952.**

*The original Proclamation of the Accession of Queen Elizabeth in 1952 signed by the then Mayor, Thomas Sandland.*

*Elizabeth Court in April 1999.*

## ENGLAND'S LANE

Mrs Vivienne Evans suggests this is likely to be a corruption of "Inlands" which refers to a lane leading to open land within the boundary of the original Borough of Dunstable known as Great and Little Inland . Early maps of the town show that Britain Street, prior to its being made up in 1910/11, was also referred to as England's Lane. The name was also chosen by the British Land Company to describe the town's very first housing estate, The Englands Estate (see St Peters Road).

*England's Lane in April,1999.*

# GRAHAM ROAD

R Parker Graham was the second headmaster of the Wesleyan School from 1900 to its demise by fire in 1908. He later became the first headmaster of Britain Street (now Priory) school after "3 years in limbo", in 1911. He served on the Council for a total of 32 years and was elected Mayor in 1912.

*Councillor R Parker Graham in his Mayoral Robes.*

*Graham Road in 1963.*

# GREAT NORTHERN ROAD

Follows the path of an ancient track way and leads to the former Great Northern Railway Station (Dunstable Town) which opened in 1858. The road was finally made up in 1886 and the last regular passenger service ran in 1965. A vehement local campaign in the 1980's and 1990's has failed to secure its reopening.

*Great Northern Road in about 1910.(BS)*

*The Fourth Dunstable Girl Guides meet in Great Northern Road prior to the 1954 Old People's Welfare Association Carnival. (LM/DG)*

*The Dunstable Sea Cadet Unit march in Great Northern Road before the 1958 Carnival.(LM/DG)*

# GROVE ROAD

A rural sounding partner for Park Road. Like its neighbours, Downs Road and Borough Road, it was not made up in its early years and Dorothy Allen, whose family moved into their home built by Arthur Robinson in 1916, remembers it as very muddy and Wellington boots were a necessity in winter.

*Grove Road in 1999.(BS)*

# HALF MOON LANE

Named after the Half Moon Inn, a building which still stands on the opposite side of London Road. The lane follows part of the upper route of the ancient Icknield Way which continued in a straight line to the top of Dunstable Downs, the western section only remaining as a public footpath. The Lane originally formed the boundary of Bedfordshire and Hertfordshire, the Parishes of Caddington and Kensworth only transferring to Bedfordshire on the creation of County Councils as administrative bodies in 1888.

*Half Moon Lane Coronation Street party in June 1953. (BT)*

*Half Moon Lane in 1958 before it was made up as a publicly maintained highway, showing "agger" of the Romanised Icknield Way.*

# HILLSIDE ROAD

An unimaginative name for a road close to the side of Blows Downs which links the Downside Estate with Sundown Avenue.

*Maisonettes at the junction of Hillside Road and Mayfield Road in about 1960*

# HOLLAND COURT

Built on the site of Holland's Dairy.

# HOWARD PLACE

There are several members of the Howard Family living in the very near vicinity of this road but they have generously acknowledged that it is not named after them, but after the Howards of Bedford who were prison reformers, philanthropists and industrialists.

# JARDINE WAY

William Jardine, a Draper of High Street North, was one of the 16 original Burgesses elected to the modern Borough Council in March 1865. He served as Mayor from 1869-70.

*Alderman William Jardine in 1869.*

# KING STREET

The first road to be made up by the Borough Council (in 1882) under new powers granted under the Public Health Act 1875.

*King Street in 1999.*

# LINCOLN CLOSE

When South Bedfordshire District Council was constructing this extension to the Downside Estate in 1976, it consulted the Dunstable Charter Trustees (the body which prior to the re-establishment of a separate Town Council in 1985 was charged with preserving the Mayorality and civic traditions of the town) on suitable street names. They responded by suggesting a list of English county names, three of which were subsequently adopted - Lincoln, Suffolk and Norfolk.

# LONG HEDGE

A traditional field name retained for the access road to the Priory Park development which includes the following three street names:

## ASH GROVE     ## LIME WALK     ## OAK CLOSE

*Three views of the Priory Park development off Long Hedge in 1999. (BS)*

# LOVERS WALK

I have heard several suggested romantic origins for this name but have been unable to find any hard evidence to support any of them.

*Lovers Walk in 1999.*

# MANSHEAD COURT

Manshead is the old hundred, or Saxon administrative unit, which included part of Dunstable.

# MAYFIELD ROAD

A pastoral name selected in common with other roads in the vicinity. May is certainly in abundance on nearby Blows Down.

*The Green in Mayfield Road in February 1961. The area has been cleared of trees but has not yet been formally laid out as a grassed area. (BT)*

# MORCOM ROAD

Dr Augustus Morcom was a family doctor in the late 19th century who lived at Montpelier House in High Street South. He was Medical Officer of Health to Luton Rural District Council and Mayor of Dunstable in 1890-91.

*Dr Augustus Morcom in his Mayoral Robes in 1890.*

*The Morcom Road flats in March 1961. (BT)*

## MOUNTVIEW AVENUE

Looks over to the slopes leading to Kensworth Quarry, originally known as Mount Pleasant. The first houses were of an, at the time, experimental pre-cast design recommended by the Building Research Establishment in 1953. Dunstable was one of only 4 local authorities which took part in the experiment.

## OAKWOOD AVENUE

Continues the woodland theme of many roads in the area.

*Oakwood Avenue/Graham Road junction in 1976. (AM)*

*The original St Augustine's Church in Oakwood Avenue in 1987, showing the Mayfield Road bungalows in the background. The building was replaced by the present Church in 1992.*

# NEW WOODFIELD GREEN

A pastoral name selected by the Council for its major pre-cast concrete housing estate. The name gained much affection in the area and has been retained as New Woodfield Green for the new housing scheme which replaced it.

*The completed redevelopment of Woodfield Green by the South Bedfordshire Urban Development Trust Co. Limited in 1990 . (AW)*

*A montage by David Whiting Photography of Luton showing new houses in New Woodfield Green and the type of building they replaced. (AW)*

# NORCOTT CLOSE

Named after the north London builder, Norcott Building Co. Ltd, who developed this road. The company name comes from its two principals, H Norris and E H Endicott.

*The letterhead of the Norcott Building Co.*

# PARK ROAD

A neighbour for Grove Road.

*Park Road in 1999.(BS)*

# PRIORY ROAD

The present road to the east of Priory Church was laid out after 1880 to connect Richard Street with Church Street.

*Priory Road in 1999.*

*An aerial view in about 1935 showing Priory Road in the centre and the newly completed Bernard Close in the foreground. In the bottom left corner is the Bagshawe's factory (see Dukeminster Estate) whilst in the top left corner Downs Road and Blows Road are largely undeveloped, the latter leading to a newly laid out cul-de-sac which was to be Sundown Avenue containing only two properties. In the background is the Stipers Hill Estate. On the right of the picture is the Britain Street School (now Priory Middle). (LM/DG)*

# RICHARD STREET

One of the earliest roads to be laid out off the main crossroads, the origins are unclear. Possible suggestions include Richard de Morins, a 13th century Prior or King Richard I.

# ST PETER'S ROAD

Refers to the nearby Priory Church of St Peter. First developed by the British Land Company as part of its Englands Estate in the 1880's, it was formally made up and adopted as public highway in 1901.

*St Peter's Road looking towards Priory Road in about 1910.*

*A similar view in 1999.*

# SOUTHWOOD ROAD

Continuing the general wooded/pastoral themes for roads in the Downside Estate.

*Flats in Southwood Road in about 1960. (SBDC)*

*An aerial view of the Downside Estate in about 1961 showing Southwood Road on the right hand side and leading off it (from bottom to top) Mountview Avenue, Woodfield Green, Brive Road and Graham Road. Jardine Way has not yet been constructed. (DG)*

# STATION ROAD

Led to the Great Northern (Town) Railway Station.

*A View of Blows Down from the Church Street Station in about 1910.*

*The platform of the railway station looking north shortly before its closure to passenger traffic in 1965.*

## SUFFOLK CLOSE

A neighbour for Norfolk and Lincoln Closes.

## SUNDOWN AVENUE

The Nash Family, who were partly responsible for the original development of the road in the early 1930's, once lived in a property called "Sundown" at the junction of Borough Road and Howard Place. It was originally an unmade "L" shaped cul - de- sac leading off Blows Road but, following residents' representations in 1952, the Borough Council took over responsibility for its maintenance and completed the crescent layout we see today.

*Sundown Avenue as an unmade road in about 1952 looking across Half Moon Lane towards Blows Road.*

## WELLINGTON TERRACE

A splendid terrace of mid 19th century cottages which probably commemorate the First Duke of Wellington. However, he died in 1852 and the houses were already there at the time of the 1851 census.

## WOODFIELD GATE

A short section of the former Woodfield Green which now provides the entrance to the replacement development, New Woodfield Green.

# Chapter 4 - BEECROFT

## AIDANS CLOSE

Like several roads in this vicinity, the origin is unclear. The Developers originally suggested a series of names which were unacceptable to the Council. The Highways Committee asked its then Chairman, the late Alderman Wilf Lack and the Borough Engineer to report back on a more suitable set of names. The Council's Minutes record this and other names for the area approved in November 1968 but give no explanation for their origin. This road could possibly refer to St Aidan, a monk of Iona and Bishop of Lindisfarne who died in 651.

## CUSWORTH WAY/WALK, ROTHERWOOD CLOSE, SCAWSBY CLOSE

These three streets, like Aidans Close above, were also named by Alderman Lack in 1968, for reasons now unclear although Scawsby may refer to the town of the same name in Yorkshire.

*Members of the Manshead Archaeological Society carry out a rescue dig on the site of what was to become Scawsby Close. A circular ditch had been spotted from a glider and this was later revealed to be a bronze age barrow. (MAS)*

# ALDBANKS

An abbreviation of "Alderman Banks". Albert William Banks served continuously on the Borough Council from 1920 to 1952 and was Mayor of Dunstable in 1946/49. A road safety officer by profession, he was a founder of the Dunstable Old People's Welfare Association "Cordova".

*An illustration from a 1957 brochure showing "conceptions" of how the interiors of the new precast homes in Aldbanks could look.*

# ASHCROFT

Ash trees are common to the Dunstable area and "Croft" appears frequently in Dunstable street names - "Croft Green", "Pipers Croft".

*Ashcroft in April 1957. (BT).*

# AYNSCOMBE CLOSE

Thomas Aynscombe was a member of the Chew/Marsh family who were major local benefactors in the 18th Century. The family owned land in this vicinity.

*The commemorative plaque referring to Thomas Aynscombe above the entrance to Chew's House. Sadly the two bluecoat schoolboy figures were stolen in 1998. (Alan Hill)*

*The Aynscombe memorial in the Priory Church.*

# BEECH GREEN

A neighbour for "Ash" croft. Beech trees are of course common throughout the Chilterns.

*Beech Green in May 1983. (JH)*

*Beech Green in February 1999.*

# BEECHWOOD COURT

Originally a small cul-de-sac known locally as "The Banjo", off Drovers Way, with which the houses were numbered consecutively. The present road and flats were extended in 1968 by M S White (Dunstable) Ltd into the grounds of the former Beechwood House, the substantial mock Tudor style home of the late Mr Fred England. The house was appropriately named as it was surrounded by substantial beech trees.

*The original Beechwood House in 1960. (BT).*

*Beechwood Court in July 1975. (BT).*

171

*Beechwood Court nearing completion in 1968. (AW).*

# BEECROFT WAY

The whole area was originally developed and sold off as private building plots by the Beecroft family on a design by T Alwyn Lloyd, an Architect of Cardiff, in 1933/34. Only 11 houses were built prior to the Dunstable Borough Council purchasing the estate at the end of the Second World War. The Council archives in Grove House reveal the protracted and not always friendly negotiations between the parties. The earlier houses can still be clearly identified in Chiltern Road and Beecroft Way. Mr E R Beecroft presided at the opening of Waterlow Road Methodist Church. The larger Council estate was eventually started in 1946 and was developed over several phases during the next 10 years.

*Italian prisoners of war (based at the POW Camp at the London Gliding Club) dig footings at the Beecroft Estate in February 1946. (LM/DG).*

*Beecroft Way and the adjoining estate under construction in September 1947 showing in the top right corner Beechwood House, the Meadway hostel and the California Pool. In the top centre, Catchacre is still a large allotment site (RAF).*

*Beecroft Way under construction in February 1946 with Worthington Road in the background. (DG)*

*Beecroft Way Coronation street party in June 1953. (BT)*

# BENNING AVENUE

The Benning Family was as important as any in the modern development of Dunstable. Charles Stockdale Benning was first Mayor of the new Borough of Dunstable in 1865. A local Solicitor, he resigned from the Council in 1868 to become Dunstable's second Town Clerk until 1892 when he was succeeded by his son Charles Crichton Stuart Benning for the next 32 years. The family law practice is still in operation in West Street under the name Knowles Benning.

During the period of Office of C S Benning, the Council acquired the Manor of Dunstable and Market Rights from the Crown, whilst his son was primarily

*C S Benning in 1866*

responsible for the expansion of Dunstable into what was then known as Upper Houghton Regis in 1907. On his retirement, the Council Members subscribed to a portrait which hung behind the mayoral chair in the old town hall until its demolition in 1963.

*C C S Benning being bumped at a ceremony to mark the expansion of the Borough of Dunstable in 1907.*

175

*Benning Avenue in the early 1960's .(SBDC)*

# BREWERS HILL ROAD

Originally a track leading to Brewers Hill Farm. A public protest in 1891 to secure public access over the road became known locally as "the battle of Brewers Hill". After public access had been confirmed in a High Court Hearing in London, there was a grand parade and local public celebration.

*Brewers Hill Farm in February 1936. (DG)*

# BOROUGH OF DUNSTABLE.

In compliance with a Memorial received from certain Ratepayers of the Borough,
I Hereby Convene a

# PUBLIC MEETING

Of the Ratepayers, to be held in the

# TOWN HALL,
# ON WEDNESDAY, OCTOBER 15,

## At EIGHT o'clock p.m.

**For the purpose of 'Considering the means to be adopted for securing the maintenance of the Public Rights to the use of**

# BREWER'S HILL ROAD.

## W. J. HAMBLING,
### MAYOR.

October 11th, 1890.

H. BALLANS, PRINTER, DUNSTABLE.

*Notice of a public meeting in 1890 to discuss public rights of way over Brewers Hill Road.*

*Railway signal box at the Brewers Hill Road level crossing in about 1960.(BCC)*

*Brewers Hill Road/Drovers Way junction in April 1968, when it was a signposted alternative route to avoid the town centre crossroads. This designation was changed in the 1980's and a heavy lorry ban introduced into the area. (BT)*

## BRYONY WAY

A wildflower common in the hedgerows of Green Lanes in this area.

## BUNHILL CLOSE

An original field name for part of Brewers Hill Farm. A former farm worker recalled that the field on which the close was built contained a mound or hill riddled with rabbit warrens. He remembered catching many "bunnies" on the site.

## CAMPION CLOSE/IVY CLOSE

More wildflowers found in the area.

## COOKFIELD CLOSE

An original field name. The Cook family owned the adjoining Brewers Hill farm for generations.

## CREASEY PARK DRIVE

Leads to Dunstable Football Ground known as Creasey Park after a former Chairman, the well known local hotelier Mr Walter "Wally" Creasey who was Mayor of Dunstable in 1965/66. Dunstable Football Club has enjoyed a somewhat chequered career, although the highlight was undoubtedly when George Best was signed for some pre - season games played before vast crowds in 1975. The team now competes in the South Midlands League.

*Alderman Wally Creasey*

# CROFT GREEN

Many of the roads on post-war housing estates were given rural sounding names. Croft Green means an enclosed piece of arable land. It has also been suggested, however, that this name relates in some way to the BeeCROFT family who initiated development of this part of the town in the 1930s.

*Croft Green in about 1960. (SBDC)*

*Croft Green in June 1999.*

# DROVERS WAY

Replicates the original name of the ancient green highway with which it runs parallel (now known as Green Lane) over which sheep from Totternhoe were driven to market in Dunstable.

*Drovers Way in April 1968 showing, on the right, the site of Weatherby still to be developed. (BT)*

*Drovers Way looking south from the junction with Worthington Road in about 1960. (SBDC)*

*An aerial view of Drovers Way and the Beecroft Estate in about 1960. In the foreground the Meadway Court flats are under construction whilst in the background the shops, pub and church have yet to be built in Westfield Road. (DG)*

# FRANKLIN ROAD

Edward Franklin was Mayor of Dunstable in 1911/12 and 1916/18. A carpenter and joiner who ran an undertakers business in High Street South, he led the public campaign and subsequent court action known as "The Battle of Brewers Hill" which led to that road being opened to public access.

*Edward Franklin in 1911.*

*The view from Dunstable Downs in about 1920 looking towards West Street, with Franklin Road under construction in the background.*

## GREENFIELD CLOSE

Like others in the locality remembers an ancient field name of the former Brewers Hill Farm.

## HAMBLING PLACE

William James Hambling, who was Mayor in 1880-82 and 1887-90 was one of the leading citizens of his day. Headmaster of the Chews Charity School from 1856 until his sudden death in 1898, he was also Colonel of the Bedfordshire Volunteers, Church Warden of the Priory Church and President of the Dunstable Institute. His son Sir Herbert Hambling was made a Freeman of the town in 1924. Two other sons emigrated to Canada where they established the community of Dunstable in Alberta.

*Mayor W J Hambling in 1890.*

*The Hambling Memorial in the Priory Church.*

TO THE MEMORY
OF
LT-COL.WILLIAM JAMES HAMBLING, J.P.
BORN 1831 – DIED 1898
HIS SON
SIR HERBERT HAMBLING, BARONET
GAVE A GENEROUS DONATION
TOWARDS THE RESTORATION OF
THE TOWER OF THIS CHURCH IN
1930

## HILLCROFT

An original field name as in Ashcroft.

# LANGRIDGE COURT

John Langridge, a grocer in High Street South, was Mayor in 1886-87 whilst his brother Arthur was Mayor on four occasions between 1894 and 1902. He represented Dunstable at the Coronation of Edward VII.

*John and Arthur Langridge in Mayoral Robes.*

# LAWRENCE WAY

This industrial area is named after the developer, Walter Lawrence.

# LORING ROAD

Sir Nigel Loring, who was referred to as one of the greatest warriors of his day and was Chamberlain to the Black Prince, was a 14th century benefactor to the Priory Church. He died in 1386 and was buried at Chalgrave, the family Seat.

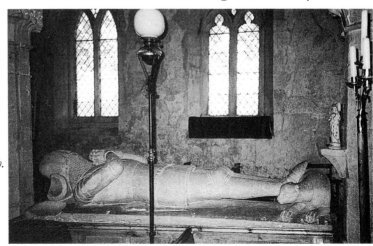

*The tomb of Sir Nigel Loring in Chalgrave Church.*

# MAIDENBOWER AVENUE

Maiden Bower, a Neolithic causewayed camp which was re-fortified during the late Iron age is one of the most significant ancient monuments in the Dunstable area. Situated between north Dunstable and Sewell, the Maiden Bower is 700 ft in diameter and the original earthworks are now topped by a line of trees which are best viewed from the open land at the junction of Hillcroft and Weatherby.

*The Maidenbower Avenue/Westfield Road junction in about 1960. (SBDC)*

*An aerial view of Maiden Bower in the late 1950's. (MAS)*

# NORMAN WAY

Like its neighbour, Saxon Close, it adjoins the Green Lanes ancient Green Highway, leading across the parish of Totternhoe.

# NORTH STATION WAY

Access off Brewers Hill Road leading to new South Bedfordshire District Council offices and several factories which were built on the site of Dunstable North Station.

*Dunstable North Station in about 1890.*

*HRH the Duke of Gloucester opens the new District Council Offices on the site of the North Station in September 1989 watched by the Chairman of the Council, Mrs Isobel Beesley. (SBDC)*

*Dunstable North Station and Gas Works in 1963 with Brewers Hill Road running through the centre of the picture.*

# ORCHID CLOSE

Like many other roads in the area - named after well known chalk habitat plants found in the area. Wild orchids still grace Dunstable Downs and Totternhoe Knolls.

# PASCOMB ROAD

Named in 1951 after the nearby Pascomb Pit on Dunstable Downs which was the site of the renowned Orange Rolling. The name is believed to be derived from the Pasque flower, now a rare chalkland plant and Coomb, a dry valley.

*Orange rolling on Pascomb Pit in the late 1930's. (DG)*

# REDFIELD CLOSE

Retains an original field name of the Brewers Hill Farm.

# SAXON CLOSE

See Norman Close

# SPINNEY CRESCENT

The adjoining Spinney in Green Lanes is still evident today.

*An aerial view of the Beecroft Estate in about 1960 showing Spinney Crescent in the foreground. (SBDC)*

# WEATHERBY

Originally the site of the Meteorological Office weather forecasting station, which moved to Bracknell in Berkshire in 1956. The site was divided into a series of building plots, the largest of which was sold to the builders George Wimpey for £225,000.

*The Meteorological Office pylons in July 1952 viewed from Totternhoe Road prior to the construction of Lancot Lower School. (BT)*

# WESTFIELD ROAD

A companion name for Northfields and Southfields, the road was first started in 1935 as a private development off the A5. An advertisement by Janes Builders for the first houses appeared in the Dunstable Gazette in August 1935. It was later extended considerably in the 1950's as part of the Brewers Hill Council housing development.

*Westfield Road Coronation street party in June 1953. (BT)*

*Westfield Road shops in 1963.*

*Westfield Road shops in 1999.*

*Westfield Road and the Eight Bells Public House viewed from St Fremunds Church.*

# WORTHINGTON ROAD

Worthington G Smith, historian, illustrator, botanist and author, was made the first Freeman of Dunstable in 1903. The achievements of the multi-talented Dunstablian are only now being properly recognised and a commemorative plaque has been placed near the site of his cottage in High Street South.

*Worthington George Smith in 1899.*

*Worthington Road in 1976. (AM)*

*Worthington Road in 1976. (AM)*

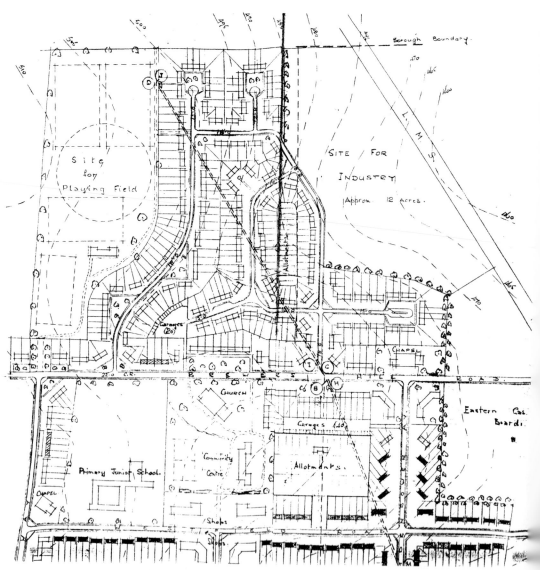

*The original plan submitted by Dunstable Borough Council to Bedfordshire County Council in July 1953 for the extension of the Beecroft Estate into Westfield Road and Brewers Hill Road. Note the initial plan for a church in Brewers Hill Road and for shops on all four corners of the junction of Westfield Road and what was to become Ashcroft.*

# Chapter 5 - NORTH DUNSTABLE

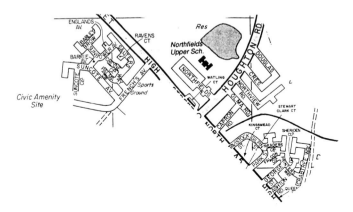

When Henry I established the modern town of Dunstable about 1109, he endowed land from the royal manor of Houghton Regis. As Dunstable has expanded over the years, it has continued to absorb parts of Houghton and other surrounding villages. Most of North Dunstable covered by this Chapter remained part of Houghton Regis until 1907 and was known as " Upper Houghton" and a large part of the estate off French's Avenue was not added within the town boundary until April 1985.

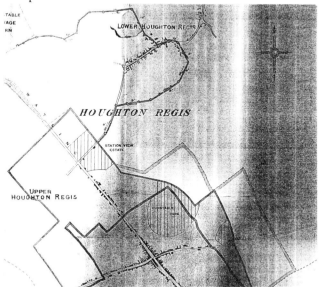

*The incorporation of Upper Houghton into Dunstable in 1907 was most controversial at the time , the various parties only agreeing once Dunstable Borough Council undertook to connect the new area to the Town's sewage works and also to provide a link for draining the main village of Houghton Regis (then known as Lower Houghton). This is a copy of the original Boundary Order Map showing the extended boundary and, in the top, the line of the new sewer.*

# ASHTON ROAD

Mrs Frances Ashton, daughter of Thomas Chew, was one of the great 18th Century benefactors to Dunstable. The Ashton Schools Foundation was endowed by her and provided the adjoining School, originally Ashton Grammar School, now Ashton Middle School. The endowment today includes Ashton St Peter Lower School and Manshead School. The large house in this street "Ashton Lodge" was originally the Preparatory School for the Grammar School.

# BARLEY BROW

A developer's suggestion.

*Barley Brow in 1999. (PH)*

# BARRIE AVENUE

It has been suggested it was named after J M Barrie, author of "Peter Pan", but the connection with Dunstable is unclear.

*Barrie Avenue in April 1999. (PH)*

# CAPRON ROAD

With the adjoining Olma Road was originally part of the "Station View" estate. Roads of this name appear in several towns at the turn of the century but its origin is unclear. I have also been told that at the time the road was laid out, it originally only contained the premises of Marsh and Young, Iron Foundry. When a name for the new road was being sought, something resembling a hat stand was found amongst the scrap metal on the premises which appeared to contain some form of armorial bearings and the letters "capron". This was therefore put forward as a possible road name and duly accepted. There is, however a road of the same name in Luton which, like its Dunstable counterpart is next to a railway station so this may be another possible explanation.

## MARSH & YOUNG
**━ IRONFOUNDERS ━**

### Capron Road, Dunstable

*An advertisement for Marsh and Young Iron Founders in 1939.*

Engineers' Castings of good quality

PROMPT DELIVERIES     ::     COMPETITIVE PRICES

Send us your enquiries     ●     'Phone Dunstable 89

*Capron Road in 1996. (JS)*

# CHEYNE CLOSE

Like other roads in this locality, probably refers to areas of London, this time, Cheyne Walk in Chelsea.

*Cheyne Close in 1999. (PH)*

# DOUGLAS CRESCENT

Just over the border in the town of Houghton Regis, this road was constructed by the local developers, Mead Estates and named after Douglas, the youngest son of William Mead.

*Mead Estates' advertisment for new houses in Douglas Crescent in 1939.*

# ENGLAND'S AVENUE

Not to be confused with England's Lane in the Priory area. It is most unusual to find two streets with such similar names at opposite ends of the town especially as this contravenes the normal conventions for street naming. This was probably permitted in our case as England's Avenue was originally part of Houghton Regis and not transferred to Dunstable until 1985. The England Family owned land in this vicinity.

*England's Avenue in 1999.(PH)*

# FRENCH'S AVENUE

Refers to French's Farm to which it once led. What is now Salters Way and the adjoining Closes were for many years known as the French's Gate Allotments, which, when developed, were marketed as The French's Gate Estate.

# GEORGE STREET

Originally led to the distinctive gates and clock tower of Waterlows Printing Works. The road was laid out in 1889 and it has been suggested to be in the honour of the then Prince George who was crowned King George V in 1910. This and other roads were laid out to accommodate print workers moving from London and why one of these on the opposite side of High Street North was named Waterlow Road and not this one is unclear.

*The entrance to Waterlow Print Works in George Street in 1988. (DG)*

199

*A young lad, later identified as Mr Hull , delivering milk in George Street in about 1920. (DG)*

*Apprentice John Summerfield being wheeled out of the George Street entrance to Waterlows in a traditional ceremony "after serving his time" in April 1955. (BT)*

# GILPIN CHASE/STREET

Possibly named after Sir Richard Thomas Gilpin, a trustee of the Chews Charity School who died in 1870 or more likely, after Col. Gilpin, the local Member of Parliament who supported the petition leading to the grant of the 1864 Borough Charter.

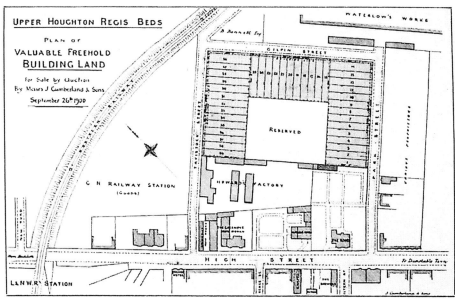

*The original sale plan of building plots in Gilpin Street.*

# HOUGHTON PARADE

An appropriate name for a parade of shops on the corner of Houghton Road and High Street North

*Houghton Parade in June 1955. (BT)*

## HOUGHTON ROAD

The road leading to Houghton Regis from the A5, it appears in early Directories as "Mixt Way", a name Mr Fred Moore remembers some of his older customers still using.

*Construction of the roundabout to replace traffic lights at the Houghton Road/High Street North Roundabout in May 1978.(DG)*

*Councillor J T Dales (see Dale Road) complaining of the condition of "Mixt Way" in 1912.*

# NORTHFIELDS

A major Council housing development on former fields and allotments on the northern boundary of the town. The Estate was completed in 1935 and on January 13th the following year the adjacent Northfields School was opened. The original plans for the Estate were extended to accommodate workers moving from Birmingham when AC Sphinx Spark Plug Co. moved to Watling Street. It has been suggested that the company were originally located in an area known as Northfield in Birmingham but the extensive files on the negotiations to secure their relocation in Dunstable do not support this theory.

*Northfields VE Day party in May 1945. (DG)*

*Northfields looking south east in May 1983. Two of the properties on the left were later destroyed by fire and have now been replaced with new houses. (JH)*

## OLMA ROAD

A lovely story lies behind this name. I am told the Developer, Arthur Carter, had 4 children, Olive, Leonard, Mary and Albert and named the road after their initial letters. Mr Carter was also responsible for the first development in Suncote Avenue, Barrie Avenue and Garden Road from 1934 onwards.

## PALMA CLOSE

The reason is uncertain, but it may refer to the principal town on the Spanish island of Majorca.

## PARK STREET

The area behind Ashton Middle School and Grove House Gardens, to which this road would once have led and which now includes the site of Dunstable College and the Leisure Centre, all formed part of Dunstable Park. For the same connection an important nearby farmhouse on High Street North was called "Park Farm".

*Park Street in January 1990 looking towards the now demolished Waterlow's Factory. (DB)*

*The same view two years later following the demolition of the factory and its replacement with the Printers Way Estate. (DB)*

# PRINTERS WAY

This 1990's development off George Street reflects the fact that the site was for most of this century the principal base of the renowned printers Waterlow & Sons Limited.

Waterlows moved their printing and book binding departments to Dunstable in 1891 and soon became the town's largest employer. Over the years the factory buildings expanded considerably and, at their peak before the 2nd World War, employed 1,700 persons. There were various Departments including envelopes and various security printing processes such as bank notes and postage stamps. The company also provided outstanding recreational facilities which, in later years, were enjoyed by the wider community. Modern hi-tec printing processes rendered such large works redundant and the company relocated to much smaller new pemises in Foster Avenue on the Woodside Park Industrial Estate and the George Street premises were demolished for housing development in 1995.

## CRABTREE WAY

## FALCON CLOSE

## SHERIDEN CLOSE

These three streets on the Printers Way estate, all recall particular types of printing presses used by the company at its Dunstable works in its hey day.

## READERS CLOSE

On the site of the Readers Department of the former Waterlow Printing Works.

*Waterlow's Bank Note department. (MP)*

# PUBLIC NOTICE.

In view of the possibility of an AIR RAID, the Local Emergency Committee have arranged with Messrs. WATERLOW & SONS that, on receiving notice of the approach of hostile aircraft, a signal shall be given by

# THREE BLASTS OF 30 SECONDS EACH
## OF THEIR WORKS HORN,

repeated after One Minute interval. On this being given Householders must AT ONCE extinguish all lights in their houses visible from the outside.

It is essential that attention should be given to this notice, and no light should be shown after the signal has been given.

The Committee wish to impress upon the Public that, from this date, all windows, BACK and Front, Skylights and Fanlights must be effectively obscured. Window Blinds, made of cream, yellow, or other light coloured material do not comply with the Home Office Order.

Flashlights when used in the streets must show a light on the ground only.

Persons disobeying these orders incur the risk of heavy Penalties.

In case of an Air Raid persons should remain indoors.

Dated this 18th day of February, 1916.

For the Committee,

## FRED. T. GARRETT, Mayor,
CHAIRMAN.

The Town Hall, Dunstable.

Waterlow & Sons Limited, Printers, Dunstable and London.

*Waterlow's provided a range of public services including the use of the works' horn as an air raid signal during the First World War. (MP)*

*The demolition of Waterlow's main factory entrance in January 1990. (DB)*

*The same view showing the completed Printers Way in July 1995. (DB)*

*Another view of the factory during demolition in January 1990. (DB)*

*The same view as the last picture but this time in July 1995 showing the junction of Printers Way and Sheriden Close. (DB)*

*The site of Waterlow's Pump House and pond in January 1990. (DB)*

*The same view showing the completed Crabtree Close in July 1995. (DB)*

## QUEENS COURT

A modern private flats development built on the site of Flinte House. The Council wished to name it "Flint Court" but the developers were unimpressed and selected this alternative which is, presumably, a companion for nearby Queensway.

*Queens Court in 1985. (BCC)*

## RAVENSCOURT

Like other roads nearby, is probably named after London locations; this time, Ravenscourt Park.

## SALTERS WAY

Built in 1969 this road followed the line of an ancient sock (or salt) way which passed over Puddle Hill to the west of Watling Street. The ancient path still exists as a public footpath to Sewell leading to the end of Salters Way.

*A newspaper advertisement for what was to become Salters Way in 1969. The three bedroomed town house shown was priced at £4,650.*

## SUNBOWER AVENUE

The origin of this name is unclear bur one former resident believed it to be associated with the nearby Maiden Bower earthworks.

*Sunbower Avenue in 1999.(PH)*

## SUNCOTE AVENUE/CLOSE

Initially private roads developed by Arthur Carter in 1936 as part of "The French's Gate Estate". The reason for his choice of name is unclear.

## TAVISTOCK STREET

Reputedly laid out by the eldest son of the Duke of Bedford who carries the title Marquis of Tavistock. The Dukes of Bedford were Lords of the Manor of Dunstable until the mid 19th century.

## WATLING COURT

A flats development in the most northern section of the A5 near the junction with Houghton Road which retains the original name of this famous Roman Road leading from Dover to Anglesey in North Wales. (see also High Street North)

*The section of High Street North beyond Watling Court was traditionally known as Watling Street as illustrated in a 1930 postcard showing Kitt's Inn.*

*An aerial view of Suncote Avenue in September 1947 clearly showing, as a footpath in the centre of the picture, the route of the original Roman cutting which avoided Puddle Hill. In the right of the picture can be seen the French's Gate Allotments which were later to be redeveloped for housing and in the foreground the worked-out New World Quarry which was later filled as the town's main refuse tip and is now partly occupied by factory units and the Tidy Tip. (RAF)*

# Chapter 6 - WEST DUNSTABLE

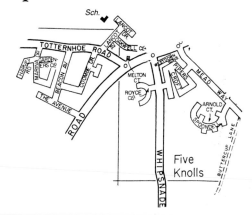

## ARNOLD COURT

Built by Robinson and White Limited and although the White family are connected to the Arnold Sand Quarry family from Leighton Buzzard, the Chairman of Arnold White Estates, Mr Colin White, has confirmed there is no connection in this instance.

## THE AVENUE

A private road developed by Mr Thomas Wass Flory of Kingscroft Estates who was responsible for much inter-War development in Dunstable. Originally called Western Avenue. The original intention was to extend the housing development westwards and a crescent of horse chestnut trees laid out for the purpose is still evident today but housing permission was refused following a public inquiry and the site is now contained within the South Bedfordshire Green Belt.

*The Avenue looking towards Tring Road in April 1964. (BT)*

# BADGERS GATE

The very latest (in 1999) street name in Dunstable. The choice reflects the fact that badgers, some originating from the adjoining Lancot Lower School, regularly patrol the area between Green Lanes and Totternhoe Road. The presence of badgers in my own front garden in Totternhoe Road confirms the point.

*Badgers Gate under construction in June 1999.*

# BEACON AVENUE

The Developers originally wished to call this road "Southern Avenue" but the Council (perhaps rightly) objected to such a name for a road in the west of the town. They suggested "Beacon" as an alternative because it looks towards Ivinghoe Beacon.

*Beacon Avenue in February 1999.*

# COOMBE DRIVE

Two alternatives have been suggested for this road. One suggestion is that it is a mis-spelling of the name of an earlier Town Clerk, John Murray Coombs. A more likely suggestion is that, like its neighbour Beacon Avenue, it refers to a dry "Coombe" on Dunstable Downs such as at "PasCOMBE".

*Coombe Drive in February 1999 overlooked by Pascombe Pit on Dunstable Downs.*

*Coombe Drive in February 1999*

# DUNSTABLE ROAD

A short section of Totternhoe Road which only transferred into the town of Dunstable in 1985 has not yet been re-named and the houses, although now part of Dunstable, still have postal addresses of Dunstable Road, Totternhoe - so it could be said that officially they reside in Dunstable Road, Dunstable!

# GARDNERS CLOSE

The original builder was Gardner Development Company.

# GREEN LANE

An ancient green highway forming part of the Totternhoe Regulated Pastures. The present name is a comparatively new colloquial name, the lane originally being known as Drovers Way, a name now replicated in the modern estate road which runs parallel to it.

*A shepherd leading his sheep to market along the old Drovers Way in about 1900.*

# HARVEY ROAD

Usually attributed to A D (Don) Harvey, who was Town Clerk of Dunstable from 1939-47 when he left to become Deputy, then Town Clerk, of Luton until 1968. He was co-author, with Borough Surveyor R F Carrington, of the war time "A Design for Dunstable" which set out in meticulous detail the foundations of the post-war expansion of the town including the Quadrant Shopping Centre and the Civic Buildings in the Queensway/Court Drive area. The road was, however, originally in the parish of Totternhoe then part of Luton Rural

*Don Harvey in about 1945.*

215

District and it is difficult to see why a Dunstable official should have been honoured. However, at the time it was built (1960) the Borough Council Minutes record that the Members were in accord with the Developers' wishes.

## HURLOCK CLOSE

Hurlock was the old name given to chalk stones used to repair roads locally. This modern development has a long history and was originally a quarry used for road building materials, later a whiting works and more recently a Council transport depot.

*Hurlock Close in February 1999.*

## LANCOT AVENUE

The hill leading to Totternhoe has traditionally been known as Lancot Hill and is perhaps a corruption of "Lambscot". A connection with Lancotbury House in Totternhoe has also been suggested but that particular property was known as Church End Farm when the housing estate in Dunstable was first laid out.

*Lancot Avenue in 1956 prior to its being formally made up as an adoptable highway. The entrance to Oakwell Drive is now on the right hand side of the picture. (BT)*

216

# LANCOT DRIVE

See previous entry.

*Lancot Lower School in Lancot Drive under construction in January 1969. (DG)*

# MARINA DRIVE

Several people have suggested this was named after Marina, the late Duchess of Kent. During the development an important Saxon burial site was uncovered from which many artifacts, including a coin hoard, are now on display in Luton Museum.

*Members of the Manshead Archaeological Society including Laurie Newman, Dennis King, Eric Bishop and Phil Pratt working on the Marina Drive burial site in August 1952 watched by interested local residents.(MAS)*

*Some of the graves found at the Marina Drive site.(MAS)*

# MEADWAY

Follows the line of an ancient British trackway. The land was originally owned by Percy Mead, a poultry farmer and Joseph Mead, a blacksmith and was known locally as "Mead's Meadows". Local builders, Mead Estates, who are related to these gentlemen built only one house in the road which was in the main developed by Kingcroft Estates in 1935 when they referred to the street by two words - "Mead Way".

*Meadway looking towards Canesworde Road in April 1975. (BT)*

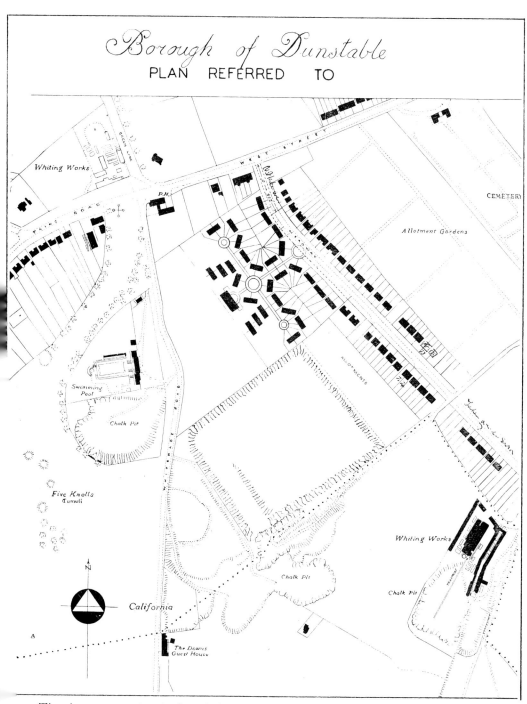

*The plan accompanying the formal Agreement to adopt Meadway as a publicly maintainable highway in June 1950. The plan also shows the Rifle Volunteer Public House (West Down Gardens), the Whiting Works (Hurlock Close), Meadway Hostel, (Pipers Croft), Spoondell Chalk Pit (Spoondell) and the California Pool (Royce Close).*

# MELTON COURT

Percy James (Jim) Melton was Mayor in 1961-62.

*Jim Melton in 1961.*

*The junction of Tring Road and Totternhoe Road prior to the construction of Melton Court in about 1970. (BT)*

*The completed Melton Court development in July 1975. (BT)*

# OAKWELL CLOSE

A possible connection with Oakwell Park at Thorn. This was one of three names offered by the Borough Council to the Developer in 1956. The others being Knoll Close and Spoondell Close.

*Oakwell Close in 1999*

*Oakwell Park, Thorn. (BS)*

# PIPERS CROFT

Originally the site of a Wartime prefabricated development built by the National Service Hostels Corporation to accommodate 91 essential workers and their families. Officially known as Meadway Hostel many local people still referred to it by the original field name, Bennetts Close. The hostel closed in 1955 and in later years accommodated former Italian prisoners of war who had been previously based at a camp within the grounds of the London Gliding Club in Tring Road. The present name was selected by the developers of the present houses, Comden and Wakelin.

*The Meadway Hostel in 1953 on the site of what is now Pipers Croft, viewed from the former California Chalk Pit, then in the process of being filled to form the car park to the California Ballroom. (BT)*

*An aerial view of Pipers Croft shortly after its completion in 1969 showing the California Pool and Ballroom and the still working Spoondell Quarry. (DG)*

# ROYCE CLOSE

Eric Royce was Mayor of Dunstable in 1971-73. He died shortly before this redevelopment of the former California Ballroom and Swimming Pool for residential purposes was completed by McLean Homes in 1980.

*Alderman Eric Royce*

*The California Swimming Pool in the summer of 1951 showing in the background the Meadway Hostel. (BT)*

*Go-karting at the former California Quarry in April 1960. (BT)*

*After its closure as a swimming pool the California was briefly used for car storage in July 1975. (BT)*

*Royce Close development on the site of the California Ballroom in 1995.*

CALIFORNIA FIESTA PRESENT 1st **GRAND PROFESSIONAL**

# BOXING SHOW

Under License of the British Boxing Board of Control

AT THE

## CALIFORNIA POOL BALLROOM

WHIPSNADE ROAD —— DUNSTABLE

'Phone Dunstable 214

## THURSDAY, JUNE 9th, 1960

Doors open 7. p.m. for 7.45 p.m.

Matchmaker: Jack King                    Promoter: Eddie Green

For the first time in Bedfordshire, at enormous expense, we present an all star programme, featuring the official British & Empire Champion Heavyweight. THREE ROUNDS BOXING BETWEEN

# HENRY COOPER & JIM COOPER

(BELLINGHAM)

GREAT SPECIAL MIDDLEWEIGHT ATTRACTION        8 (3 min.) ROUNDS CONTEST 11st. 6lbs.

# JOHNNY BERRY v DAVE GEORGE

(HARLESDEN). A protege of Terry Downes. Beaten the following—Johnny Bowler, Paul Gormley, Tony Ratcliffe, etc. Contender for area title Honours.

(WOKING). Great Tough Battler. Record: Teddy Haynes, Charlie Fordham, Tommy Lee, Tommy Power, etc.

GREAT SPECIAL 6 (3 min.) ROUNDS WELTERWEIGHT CONTEST at 10st. 7lbs.

# BERNARD HART v TERRY THOMPSON
(ELTHAM)                    (GLOUCESTER)

INTERESTING 6 (2 min.) ROUNDS MIDDLEWEIGHT CONTEST at 11st. 6lbs.

# JOE BELL v IVOR EVANS
(WEST INDIES)               (BOURNEMOUTH)

IMPORTANT 6 (3 min.) RDS. MIDDLEWEIGHT CONTEST at 11st. 4lbs.

# Tony FRENCH v Joe SUMMERVIELE
(WOKING'S STYLISH BOXER)        (BERKHAMSTED)    Good Record

SPECIAL 6(3 min.) ROUNDS HEAVYWEIGHT CONTEST

# SID CAIN v ABE STANLEY
(WATFORD'S WELL KNOWN BATTLER)        (BOURNEMOUTH)    Grand Crowd Pleaser

PRICES : Special Ringside Seats £2-2-0

Ringside £1-5-0, Reserved 17/6, 12/6, Unreserved 7/6, 5/-

LARGE CAR PARK                    2 LICENSED BARS.  LARGE NEW HALL

TICKETS from: FARMERS, LUTON & DUNSTABLE, BUCKMASTERS LTD., LEIGHTON BUZZARD.

W. F. BUNKER & CO., Printers, Luton.

*The California Ballroom is best remembered today as the venue for pop and rock concerts featuring such artists as the Rolling Stones, Diana Ross and David Bowie. However, it also staged boxing tournaments and above is an advertisement for the first, with Henry Cooper topping the bill.*

# SPOONDELL

This local authority housing development was constructed in the mid 1970's on the site of the former Spoondell chalk quarry. The area covered by the present estate and extending to the south between Whipsnade Road and Buttercup Lane was originally common land known as Spoondale Furlong. The dictionary of Hertfordshire field names (this area was until 1888 part of that county) suggests that the name comes from a "spon" or wood chip or splinter of the type later used in roofing shingle.

*Spoondell in April 1983. (JH)*

# TOTTERNHOE ROAD

Originally known locally as Lancot Hill, this name is remembered in the adjoining Avenue and Drive.

*The Downs Post Office at No. 35 Totternhoe Road. Date unknown. (DB)*

*Unusually high volumes of traffic for a Sunday morning in Totternhoe Road on 25th November 1973 occasioned by the opening of a new Sunday market at Wellhead which attracted over 15,000 people. (BT)*

*A more customary solitary scene in Totternhoe Road in 1973. (BT)*

# TRING ROAD

Leads to Tring in Hertfordshire.

*West Street Downs, Dunstable.*

*Tring Road viewed from Totternhoe Road with the Dunstable Downs (minus trees and scrub) in the early 1930's.*

*The junction of Tring Road and Whipsnade Road in 1950. (LM/DG)*

*The same junction in 1970 showing the construction of the new roundabout. This was one of the first then experimental mini-roundabouts introduced by the Road Research Laboratory. (LM/DG)*

## WESTDOWN GARDENS

Built by McCann Homes in 1986 on the site of the former Windsock and Rifle Volunteer Public Houses, I confess to being partially responsible for this rather uninspired name derived from West Street and The Downs.

*A winter scene looking from the Rifle Volunteer up the slope of Dunstable Downs in about 1910.*

*The Rifle Volunteer in the course of demolition in October 1969. (DG)*

*The Windsock Public House with its distinctive roof in about 1970.(DG)*

*Westdown Gardens in about 1995.*

# WHIPSNADE ROAD

The road leading across Dunstable Downs to Whipsnade. The area of the group of buildings on the left hand side of the hill leading from Dunstable (now known as White Rock Cottages) was traditionally known as California (see also California Ballroom, now Royce Close). There are many instances of small outlying developments around the country being called California and there is a theory that this may be associated with the 1849 Gold Rush to California, USA, which was at the time regarded as an outlying location.

*Teeing-off at the original Club House of Dunstable Downs Golf Club in Whipsnade Road (now White Rock Cottages) in 1907. (DG)*

*The former Golf Club House in 1953 (by now the Downs Guest House) showing in the background the Meadway Hostel. (BT)*

*The Dunstable Downs Golf Club initially covered land on both sides of Whipsnade Road. Here is pictured the 9th Green on the west side of Whipsnade Road in 1920. The Green is still visible just south of the present entrance to the Golf Club.(LM/DG)*

*Motor traffic attracted to the Dunstable Downs car park in Whipsnade Road on a Bank Holiday in the 1930's.(LM/DG)*

*A snow scene in Whipsnade Road by Dunstable Downs Golf Club in March 1952. (BT)*

# Chapter 7 - EAST DUNSTABLE

## ALLENBY AVENUE

Field Marshall Allenby led the victorious entry into Jerusalem in the First World War in which divisions of the local Yeomanry took part.

## BRANDRETH AVENUE

The Brandreth Family were Lords of the Manor of Houghton Regis whose Seat was at Houghton Hall. This part of Dunstable, like many others, was originally part of the Parish of Houghton Regis.

## BUCKWOOD AVENUE

Buckwood was a large wood on the Watling Street near Markyate, owned by Dunstable Priory. Many roads in the east of Dunstable have Priory connections.

## CALCUTT CLOSE

A Hamlet of Houghton Regis (see Brandreth). Calcutt House was demolished in 1975 but the remains of its medieval moat can still be seen south of Thorn. All that remains of the hamlet today is Calcutt Farmhouse. Calcutt is recorded in 1224 as "Caldecote" a name meaning "Cold Cottage", often used as a roadside shelter for travellers.

*Calcutt Farmhouse in 1999. (BS)*

## CARTERWEYS

The name "Carteswaye" appears as a highway on the 1540/43 rent list.

## CRESTA CLOSE

Suggested to be named after the Vauxhall car model of the same name.

## DALE CLOSE/ROAD

Made up as an adopted highway in 1936 at a cost of £984. 17. 2d. Very many people have suggested the name refers to the remarkable father and daughter who ran the well known Dales Dubbin Company in Tavistock Street. As Mr Dales died in 1934 shortly before the road was started, this is feasible but the spelling, however, casts doubt on this. Nevertheless, the Dales of any local worthies surely merit a street being named after them.

JT (Jonty) Dales was an independent and philanthropic member of the community who lived in the Tower House which dominated the east side of High Street North opposite Chiltern Road. He was Mayor in 1919 whilst his daughter Lucy was the first Lady Mayor of Dunstable in 1925.

First Prize Decorated Car, representing Peace
(Designed by Mr. E. Dutton)

Produced by Councillor and Miss Dales for the

DUNSTABLE PEACE PAGEANT, July, 1919

*The cover of the official Christmas greetings card sent by J T and Miss Lucy Dales as Mayor and Mayoress in 1919 showing their entry in the Peace Pageant earlier that year. The Mayor is the gentleman in the front with the beard whilst it is believed that Lucy Dales is the figure of Peace at the top of the tableau.*

# DUNCOMBE DRIVE

William Duncombe, a wealthy local merchant, in his will of 1603 endowed Charities for the relief of poverty in Dunstable, Leighton Buzzard, Hockliffe and Great Brickhill where the local inn is still known as "The Duncombe Arms".

# EVELYN ROAD

I have been told this was named after the wife of a member of the Brandreth Family of Houghton Hall who owned all the land in this vicinity. I am very grateful to Mrs Vivienne Evans for advising that it was probably Evelyn Frances Christabel Lawton of Cheshire, who married Henry Chernock Gibbs Brandreth in 1879. The first houses developed in this road were built by the Royal British Legion on land acquired from the Brandreth family, to accommodate the families of distressed ex-servicemen after the First World War . They were generally known as "The Legion Estate" and were the first residential properties to be built in the east of the town.

# FAIRFIELD CLOSE/ROAD

Named after the developer, Fairfield Estates.

*Fairfield Road under construction in 1976. (DG)*

# GOLDSTONE CRESCENT

I have been told that "Cro" gold or Cro stone, a type of fools gold of iron pyrite can be found in the chalk locally. The geology department at Luton University have confirmed that this is a distinct possibility.

## GORHAM WAY

Most roads in this vicinity have connections with Dunstable Priory. Robert de Gorham was a 12th century schoolmaster who later became Abbot of St Albans. He produced a miracle play about St Katherine believed to be the earliest recorded performance of a play in England, so enabling Dunstable to boast of being the birthplace of English dramatic art.

## HADRIAN AVENUE

Constructed in 1953, this was the principal road of the Hadrian Estate which was opened by the then Mayor, Alderman W H Robinson in September 1953. It is suggested the name refers to the Roman Emperor who lived from 76-138 AD.

*An aerial view of Commer Cars' factory in Boscombe Road in 1955 showing in the background the recently completed Hadrian Avenue and a section of Duncombe Drive leading off it but the rest of the roads in this area have yet to be developed.*

*Hadrian Avenue in 1999.*

# HIGHFIELDS COURT

Built on the site of Highfields Junior School which closed in July 1983 and was finally demolished in March 1986.

*Highfields School in Evelyn Road.(DB)*

# HOLLIWICKE ROAD

Retains the name of an ancient Dunstable street which once stood on the site of the St Mary's Gate Car Park (see Chapel Walk).

*Holliwicke Road in May 1999.*

# HOLMWOOD CLOSE

No suggestion, although holm oaks are not uncommon in the Chilterns.

# JEANSWAY

The earliest houses in the section near Dale Road were known as Aubrey Road until August 1955. Another section of the road nearer to the town centre was started in 1938 by Mr Leslie Sell and was named in memory of his first wife Jean. H C Janes & Co. extended this road and the Council agreed that the whole length be renamed "Jeansway". The three cul-de-sacs built backing onto Blows Down at that time were originally proposed to be named "Cherry Tree Close", "Russell Close" and "Crabtree Close" but the Council disagreed and ordered that the houses here be numbered consecutively with Jeansway.

*A steam roller in action laying a section of the "new" Jeansway between Kingsbury Avenue (seen on the left) and Dale Road in 1959. (JS)*

# KATHERINE DRIVE

Roads in this vicinity all have Priory connections. I am unclear whether this road refers to Katherine of Aragon (whose marriage to Henry VIII was annulled at the Priory in 1533) or St Katherine of Alexandria, who was the subject of a miracle play performed at the Priory before 1120 and believed to be one of the first recorded performances of a play in England.

It certainly does not refer to St Katherine of Genoa, after whom the United Reformed Church in this road is dedicated, as the road pre-dates the Church by several years.

The road was constructed as a dual carriageway at the request of the Council who wished to see a new and convenient access onto Poynters Road to serve anticipated large vehicle numbers from the two housing estates being developed to the north (Hadrian Estate) and south (Poynters Estate).

*Katherine Drive shopping parade in May 1999.*

*St Katherine's Church and The Sportsman Public House in Katherine Drive, May, 1999.*

*An aerial view of the Katherine Drive Estate in August 1963 with the shopping parade in the centre. St Katherine's Church has yet*

# KINGSBURY AVENUE AND GARDENS

Refers to the Royal Hunting Lodge of Kingsbury (see Kingsbury Court) but is confusing as these roads are a considerable distance away from the original Royal residence.

# LAMBS CLOSE

The developers, Robinson and White, took advice from the Council on a suitable name but the reason for this choice is now unclear. One suggestion is that this road refers to the "Ewe and Lamb" pub in Luton Road, which was for a time known locally as "Lambs"; however the road construction pre-dates the public house which replaced an earlier one of the same name in West Street. Alternatively it simply refers to the sheep which would have grazed the Blows Downs which overlook this area.

*Lambs Close in the early 1970's. (AW)*

# LINDEN ROAD AND CLOSE

A popular inter-war street name. A linden is a type of lime tree, the inner bark of which was apparently used to make doormats.

*Young mums protest at the need for a pedestrian crossing in Luton Road near the junction with Dale Road and Linden Road in June 1977. (DG)*

# LISCOMBE ROAD

The first section of the road nearest to Luton Road was developed in the 1930's by a local builder, Harry Hodges, whose wife Ruth selected the name after Liscombe Park near Leighton Buzzard. The later section of the road was built by Robinson and White Ltd.

*Mrs Margaret Hodges in the side garden of her home at number 47 Liscombe Road in the early 1950's showing open fields across to Blows Downs where Jeansway is today. (Mrs Doe)*

*Miss Susan Brown on the field path between Liscombe Road and the first few houses of Jeansway which were built at the top of Kingsbury Avenue, in 1950. (Mrs Doe)*

*Liscombe Park near Leighton Buzzard (courtesy of Sir Nicholas Bonner). (BS)*

## LOCKINGTON CRESCENT

Refers to Mary Lockington, an important 18th century benefactor of the town. With her sister Blandina Marshe she helped fund the Ladies Lodge Alms Houses in Church Street.

## LUDUN CLOSE

Takes its name from the adjoining Ludun (Luton and Dunstable) Sheltered Workshops.

*The Duke of Edinburgh opens the Ludun Workshops in 1956. (DG)*

*Staff of the Ludun Workshops celebrate their 20th Anniversary in August 1975. (BT)*

# LUTON ROAD

That part of the A505 east of the Church Street railway bridge was formally adopted as Luton Road in April, 1933.

*Luton Road looking east of the Boscombe Road junction in about 1950. (DG)*

*Luton Road looking towards the Church Street Railway Bridge in about 1950 showing, on the right Liberty's Garage (now T & H Tyres) with Bagshaw's office building in the background. On the left are the Poors Land Allotments in front of the Town Railway Station. (VM)*

*An aerial view of Luton Road in 1947 showing the British Legion houses and Highfields School in Evelyn Road as the only development on the north side with Kingsbury Avenue and the first section of Jeansway in the bottom left, Dale Road with, what was then, Aubrey Road and Allenby Avenue in the front right. (DG)*

# MARKHAM CRESCENT

Gervaise Markham was the last Prior of Dunstable serving from 1525 to 1540. It was he who handed over the Priory and its lands to the Crown and then lived in retirement in High Street South.

*The representation of Gervaise Markham, the last Prior of Dunstable in a stained glass window at the Priory Church designed by John Hayward and installed in 1972. (OR)*

*Markham Crescent in May 1999.*

## MILLERS LEY

A correspondent in the Dunstable Gazette in April 1969 suggested this road followed an ancient track which led to a stack yard where wheat and corn were stored before being taken to the mill for grinding.

## MONKS' CLOSE

Continues the Priory theme of many roads in this area although the members of the Augustinian order at Dunstable Priory were strictly Canons and not monks.

## PARROTT CLOSE

Harold Parrott was Dunstable longest serving Councillor; Mayor from 1943-46 he was the last person to be granted the Freedom of the town. On his retirement in 1967 Mr Parrott was appointed "Alderman Emeritus", an honorary Councillor for life. His son, Haydn was also Mayor in 1962. The family business, Parrott and Jackson, was close to this development in Luton Road.

*Alderman Harold Parrott making his acceptance speech in the Council Chamber at the old Town Hall, having been elected Mayor of Dunstable in 1940. (DG)*

# POYNTERS ROAD

Made up in 1930 this was a lane serving Poynters Farm and then leading on to Houghton Park. It was therefore originally called Park Road, but when a section was transferred into the Borough of Dunstable in 1933 the name was changed officially to Poynters Road to avoid confusion with the section still in Houghton Regis, which to this day is known as Park Road North.

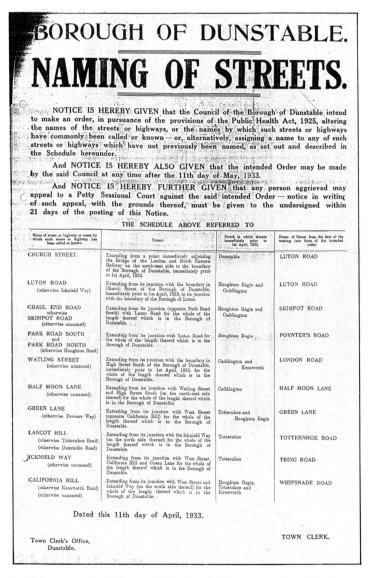

## BOROUGH OF DUNSTABLE.
## NAMING OF STREETS.

NOTICE IS HEREBY GIVEN that the Council of the Borough of Dunstable intend to make an order, in pursuance of the provisions of the Public Health Act, 1925, altering the names of the streets or highways, or the names by which such streets or highways have commonly been called or known — or, alternatively, assigning a name to any of such streets or highways which have not previously been named, as set out and described in the Schedule hereunder.

And NOTICE IS HEREBY ALSO GIVEN that the intended Order may be made by the said Council at any time after the 11th day of May, 1933.

And NOTICE IS HEREBY FURTHER GIVEN that any person aggrieved may appeal to a Petty Sessional Court against the said intended Order — notice in writing of such appeal, with the grounds thereof, must be given to the undersigned within 21 days of the posting of this Notice.

### THE SCHEDULE ABOVE REFERRED TO

| Name of street or highway or name by which such street or highway has been called or known. | Extent. | Parish in which situate immediately prior to 1st April, 1933. | Name of Street from the date of the coming into force of the intended order. |
|---|---|---|---|
| CHURCH STREET. | Extending from a point immediately adjoining the Bridge of the London and North Eastern Railway on the north-east side to the boundary of the Borough of Dunstable, immediately prior to 1st April, 1933. | Dunstable | LUTON ROAD |
| LUTON ROAD (otherwise Icknield Way) | Extending from its junction with the boundary in Church Street of the Borough of Dunstable, immediately prior to 1st April, 1933, to its junction with the boundary of the Borough of Luton. | Houghton Regis and Caddington | LUTON ROAD |
| CHAUL END ROAD otherwise SKIMPOT ROAD (otherwise unnamed) | Extending from its junction (opposite Park Road South) with Luton Road for the whole of the length thereof which is in the Borough of Dunstable. | Houghton Regis and Caddington | SKIMPOT ROAD |
| PARK ROAD SOUTH and PARK ROAD NORTH (otherwise Houghton Road) | Extending from its junction with Luton Road for the whole of the length thereof which is in the Borough of Dunstable. | Houghton Regis | POYNTER'S ROAD |
| WATLING STREET (otherwise unnamed) | Extending from its junction with the boundary in High Street South of the Borough of Dunstable, immediately prior to 1st April, 1933, for the whole of the length thereof which is in the Borough of Dunstable. | Caddington and Kensworth | LONDON ROAD |
| HALF MOON LANE (otherwise unnamed) | Extending from its junction with Watling Street and High Street South (on the north-east side thereof) for the whole of the length thereof which is in the Borough of Dunstable. | Caddington | HALF MOON LANE |
| GREEN LANE (otherwise Drovers Way) | Extending from its junction with West Street (opposite California Hill) for the whole of the length thereof which is in the Borough of Dunstable. | Totternhoe and Houghton Regis | GREEN LANE |
| LANCOT HILL (otherwise Totternhoe Road) (otherwise Dunstable Road) | Extending from its junction with the Icknield Way (on the north side thereof) for the whole of the length thereof which is in the Borough of Dunstable. | Totternhoe | TOTTERNHOE ROAD |
| ICKNIELD WAY (otherwise unnamed) | Extending from its junction with West Street, California Hill and Green Lane for the whole of the length thereof which is in the Borough of Dunstable. | Totternhoe | TRING ROAD |
| CALIFORNIA HILL (otherwise Kensworth Road) (otherwise unnamed) | Extending from its junction with West Street and Icknield Way (on the south side thereof) for the whole of the length thereof which is in the Borough of Dunstable. | Houghton Regis, Totternhoe and Kensworth | WHIPSNADE ROAD |

Dated this 11th day of April, 1933.

Town Clerk's Office, Dunstable.

TOWN CLERK.

*Public notice of the re-naming of Poynter's Road and other streets affected by the extension of the Borough of Dunstable in April 1933.*

## PYNDERS LANE

Several roads in this area refer to ancient field or track names and this seems to be in the same category but I have been unable to trace the original.

## RIDGEWAY AVENUE

Not named after the Ridgeway long distance path (as a companion for the Icknield Way off which it leads) but was named by the original Developers Messrs Brooks and Lloyd of Ridgeway, Enfield.

*Ridgeway Avenue looking towards Blows Downs in 1989. (SBDC)*

## ST CHRISTOPER'S CLOSE

It was originally proposed to call this cul-de-sac "Plaiters Close" but the name was changed to that of the adjoining Lower School which was opened in September 1958. The school name was selected by the first Headmistress, Miss Joan Horsley, following an appeal for suggestions from local children.

*St Christopher's Close in the early 1970's. (AW)*

## SKIMPOT ROAD

Originally led to Skimpot Farm, which is believed to be a corruption of St Mary's Pottery. The road is now the main access to the recreation area created in 1989 from the former Laporte's Sports and Social Club when Tesco won planning permission on Appeal for a Superstore on half of the site. The community centre on the site is now known as The Peter Newton Pavilion in memory of Councillor Peter Newton who was twice Mayor of Dunstable in 1978/9 and 1981/2 and who chaired the committee negotiating the land exchange with Tesco. He sadly died before the scheme was completed.

*Peter Newton JP*

## THE CREST

A suitable companion road for Ridgeway.

## THE RETREAT

No suggestion.

## THORNBURY

The medieval Manor at Thorn near Houghton Regis was known as Thornbury, the Manor is no longer but there is still today evidence of Thorn's moat.

## WALGRAVE ROAD

All roads in this vicinity have either a Priory or Manor of Houghton Regis connection but how this name fits into that pattern is unclear. Of no direct relevance but of some personal interest is that my own family originate from the village of Walgrave in Northamptonshire.

## WESTERN WAY

Unknown origin but rather surprising for a small cul-de-sac off Ridgeway Avenue in the eastern section of the town.

## WESTERN WAY

Unknown origin but rather surprising for a small cul-de-sac off Ridgeway Avenue in the eastern section of the town.

## WILBURY DRIVE

The reason why this name was chosen by Developers Pearce and Barker in 1955 is unclear to me. There may however be some connection with the prehistoric earthwork in Letchworth called Wilbury.

## WINGATE ROAD

The Wingate Family were Lords of the Manor of Harlington and once owned Lewsey Farm and property in Dunstable. George Wingate owned the Brotherhood House belonging to the Guild, owners of the Fairey Pall once displayed in the Priory Church, so continuing the Priory link of many roads in this area.

There is also a Wingate Road in Luton and in 1958 Luton Borough Council tried unsuccessfully to persuade their Dunstable counterpart to change the name of this road to avoid confusion.

## WOODFORD ROAD

Geoffrey of Woodford was Master Clerk of the Priory in 1210. Originally the road led of Brandreth Avenue but in 1956 the Council decided that a major route into the new estate should be named "Road" so that section of Brandreth Avenue between Luton Road and Katherine Drive was named "Woodford" Road.

# Chapter 8 - INDUSTRIAL ESTATES

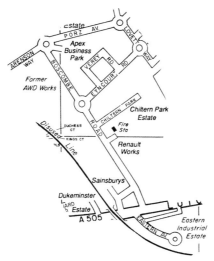

When major industry began to be attracted to Dunstable in the late 19th century, it was generally attracted to sites on the main roads on the edge of town. One of these, Bagshawe's engineering works, was also conveniently situated adjacent to the town's main railway station. By the Second World War this area had become the preferred location and it was this area which saw rapid expansion during the 1950's and 1960's followed by an almost equally rapid decline during the late 1980's from which town is only now beginning to recover.

## APEX BUSINESS CENTRE

A 1990's development of small industrial units. The name was the choice of the developer, Land and Urban.

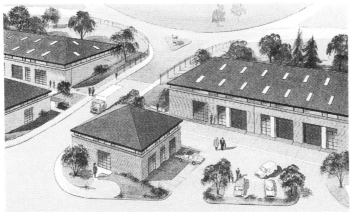

*An extract from the original sales brochure for the Apex Estate.*

# BOSCOMBE ROAD

Originally a small unadopted track containing a few houses off Luton Road. When the road was due to be extended to accommodate major industrial development, apparently residents were invited to suggest a name. I am told by the grandson of a then resident that he chose "Boscombe" because he enjoyed visits to the Dorset town of the same name where his brother lived. The road led to the Commer and Vauxhall vehicle plants and later to the Woodside Industrial Estate. Until 1999 it remained a private road with containing several well - known "sleeping policemen" but the demise of the adjoining industrial plants led to a rapid deterioration in its condition and the road was eventually made to modern highway standards with the aid of a Government grant in 1999.

*Boscombe Road showing Vauxhall Motors' Dunstable plant in 1976. (AM)*

*Boscombe Road from a similar viewpoint in February 1998 with the road surface deteriorating (DB) and in 1999 looking southwards with the road made up to modern standards.*

# Vauxhall Motors

Vauxhall's Dunstable plant in Boscombe Road started life in 1942 as a shadow factory - a precaution against bomb attack against the main factory in Luton. Initially engine parts for Churchill tanks and Bedford army trucks were produced there but after the war all commercial vehicles were manufactured here leaving the Luton plant to produce passenger vehicles. The first Dunstable built Bedford truck rolled off the newly constructed two mile production line on 2nd August 1955. By the mid 1970's the plant had expanded over 2½ million sq. ft. of floor space and its 5,700 employees were producing 83,000 Bedford Trucks a year, the highest output in Europe.

However, over capacity in the European truck market and the effects of the peace dividend following the ending of the Cold War put the plant in jeopardy and General Motors finally closed the operation in 1987. The plant was purchased by Mr David Brown who used his all wheel drive expertise to produced a revamped range of trucks but recession and a loss of army orders led to complete closure in 1992.

The resultant redundant factory contributed to Dunstable possessing the largest area of vacant industrial floor space in Europe. Regeneration of the site has been a major policy of the local councils and by 1999 parts of the site were occupied by a superstore and a retail park, with plans for an adjoining leisure park. The newer sections of the plant have been retained for industrial use. New occupiers include the headquarters of President Furniture.

*Vauxhall Motors' "DA" Block in July 1959. (VM)*

*Vauxhall Motors' "DA" Block in November 1961 showing the bridge linking it to "DB" Block. (VM)*

*Bedford Trucks main production line in December 1959. (VM)*

*Bedford Trucks main production line in February 1962. (VM)*

## Commer/Dodge/Renault

The other major vehicle manufacturing centre in Boscombe Road was that of Commer Cars' Dodge Trucks plant which became, via Rootes Chrysler and Talbot, Renault Truck Industries in 1984. Production moved from the initial Luton plant in 1955 to a new plant partly funded by the sale of some of the Company's large land holding to Vauxhall. Although part of the site still houses Renault's marketing and distribution centre, vehicle manufacture ceased on 31st March 1993, so bringing to an end Dunstable's role as a heavy vehicle manufacturing centre.

*The Dodge production line (at the time the Chrysler plant) in November 1977. (HM)*

*Renault Trucks' production line in the early 1990's. (Renault V I (UK) Ltd)*

## CHILTERN PARK

A 1990's development of warehousing built on the site of the former Renault Trucks commercial vehicle park. Dunstable falls within the Chilterns Area of natural beauty.

## DUKEMINSTER ESTATE

Built on the site of the Bagshawe's engineering works. The present estate was initially named the Fairview Trading Estate after the original developers but was re named about 1990 to reflect a change in ownership. The main occupiers are OAG Worldwide Travel (formerly ABC Travel Guides), which is one of the town's largest employers, and the Plumb Centre.

The Bagshawe Engineering Co Ltd moved to Dunstable in 1906 and rapidly became one of the town's largest employers. The company manufactured elevators and conveyors and the Bagshawe family were important local benefactors and community supporters.

*The distinctive office building of the Bagshawe engineering works in about 1930 viewed fron the Church Street railway bridge. The offices were originally built as the Fauna Building for the Festival of Empire at Crystal Palace in 1913 but were subsequently purchased by Mr Bagshawe, dismantled and re erected in Dunstable. (DG)*

*The same view as in the previous picture but taken in 1999, now showing the Dukeminster Industrial Esate and the offices of OAG.*

# EASTERN AVENUE

An obvious name for an industrial estate on the east of the town developed by H C Janes & Co in the mid 1950's.

*Parrott and Jackson's box factory east of the Town Station in 1923 on what was to become the Eastern Avenue industrial area.*

*Eastern Avenue in 1976. (AM)*

# PORZ AVENUE

Named in honour of Dunstable's German twin town, Porz am Rhein, which is today an Administrative Area within the City of Cologne. The commemorative slate plaque at the junction with Poynters Road is set in a granite block taken from the platform of the former Dunstable North Railway Station. Regular exchanges between schoolchildren and members of local societies in the two communities have taken place since 1955.

*The burgermeister of Porz, Herr Alfred Moritz, unveils the commemorative plaque re opening Porz Avenue in June 1973. The Mayor of Dunstable, Bill Farbon has his back to the camera and in the front of the onlookers is Councillor Stewart Clark (see Stewart Clark Court). (DG)*

## The Woodside Industrial Estate

For a period of 10 years from 1960, Brixton Estates developed a major industrial estate on over 100 acres of land between Boscombe Road and Poynters Road. Each of the estate roads were named after Directors of the company. The whole of the estate originally fell within the boundaries of Dunstable but the eastern secrtion (Humphreys Road) was transferred to Houghton Regis as part of boundary adjustments in 1985. A leter extension into Woodside Park (Foster Avenue) and the adjoining Houghton Hall Business Park are also in Houghton Regis.

263

*Elizabeth Frink's famous sculpture "The Flying Men" at the Porz Avenue entrance to the Woodside Industrial estate.*

*An aerial view of the Woodside Esate taken from a 1984 sales brochure showing Boscombe Road in the foreground and Eyncourt Road in the centre.*

# EYNCOURT ROAD

Named after Brixton Estates Director, Sir Gervase Tennyson D'Eyncourt.

*Eyncourt Road in 1999.*

# LOVETT WAY

Named after a Director of the Developers, Brixton Estates.

*The logo of Brixton Estates (The shape of the Company's first industrial estate in Brixton developed in 1924) looks over Lovett Way in 1999.*

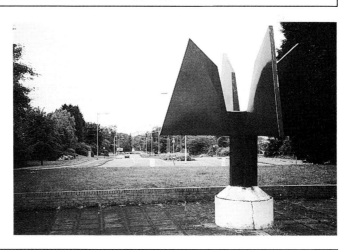

# VEREY ROAD

Michael J Verey was another Director of the Brixton Estates.

*Verey Road in 1999.*

# Chapter 9 - SOUTH WEST DUNSTABLE

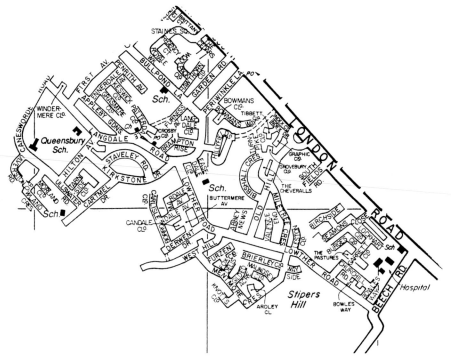

The most recent of Dunstable's residential areas which covers the gently sloping downland between Beech road, London Road and Canesworde Road. The earliest development was in Periwinkle Lane and Garden Road in the 1920's. This was followed in the late 1930's by the innovative Cottage Homestead scheme at Stipers Hill. Major development did not, however take place until the mid 1950's with the huge Croft Golf Course Estate ( now more commonly known as The Lake Disrict Estate). The Oldhill Down Estate followed shortly thereafter in 1960.

## The Croft Golf Course Estate

Plans for residential development of between 900 and 950 homes were first submitted to the Council in 1955 by Mr T C Flory for land between his existing Croft Estate (Meadway/ Canesworde Road/ First Avenue) and the Dunstable Downs Golf Course. The project was shortly taken up by Laing Homes, initially through a subsidiary company, Martin Homes. All the roads on the estate were named after locations in the Lake District and Cumbria beloved by the company founder, Sir John Laing.

The following place names appear on the map:

Carlisle
15 miles

Penrith · Brampton

Crosby · River Derwent · Skiddaw · Morland · Hilton

Appleby

Derwent Water · Keswick · Ullswater · Lowther river

Whitehaven · Shap

Patterdale

Borrowdale · Helvellyn · Caudale moor · Mardale

Ennerdale · Buttermere · Langdale · Kirkstone pass

Easedale

Scafell Pike · Wastwater

Grasmere · Ambleside · Staveley

Windermere

Ravenglass · Old Man · River Kent

Coniston Water · Tarnside · Kendal · Sedbergh

Bowland bridge

**The
Lake District
with the streets
of the Laing estate
in Dunstable**

Millom · Cartmel

Ulverston · Grange-over-Sands

O.Roucoux. Feb. 1999

Barrow in Furness · Carnforth

*A map kindly prepared by Mr Omer Roucoux showing the actual locations of all the place names in the Lake District and Cumbria found on the Croft Golf Course Estate.*

267

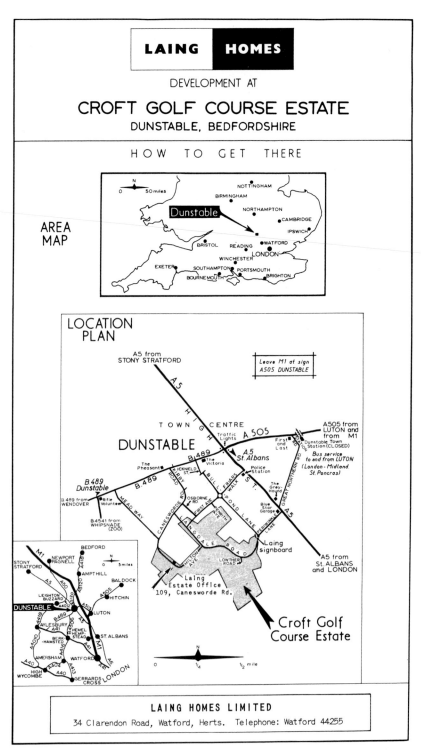

*Laing Homes' 1962 sales brochure for the Croft Golf Course Estate.*

# APPLEBY GARDENS

Small county town with railway station on the river Eden, backed by the Pennines. 14 miles south-east of Penrith, 30 miles south-east of Carlisle. Not in the Lake District National Park.

*An aerial view of Friars Walk and First Avenue, August 1961. In the top right Queen Eleanor's School stands in splendid isolation beyond the uncompleted Appleby Gardens and Lowther Road. (Aerofilms)*

# BORROWDALE AVENUE

Romantic valley stretching between the lofty peaks from about Glaramara Mountain north of Derwent Water (south of Keswick). Borrowdale is also a village, south of Keswick, in the above valley on the river Derwent.

# BOWLAND CRESCENT

There is a Bowland in Scotland, but in the Lake District we have Bowland Bridge, a hamlet 6 miles south-west of Kendal.

# BRAMPTON RISE

22 Bramptons are listed in the Bartholomew Gazetteer of the British Isles. The name means "the settlement where broom grows". Two are in Cumbria, one a small market town, 9 miles north-east of Carlisle, near the Hadrian Wall. But Laing probably thought of the other one, a small hamlet 2 miles north of Appleby.

# BUTTERMERE AVENUE

A village and lake. The village is 9½ miles south west of Keswick. The lake is 1¼ miles long. 1⅓miles wide and 329 feet above sea level, the greatest depth is 94 feet.

*An aerial view in July 1968 of Ardley Hill School showing Buttermere Avenue in the foreground.(Aerofilms)*

# CANDALE CLOSE

Unlike every other road there is no actual "Candale" in the Lake District. Research from the archives of Laing Homes who built the estate give no clue as to the reason and its seems probable that it was a simple misreading of the "u" in "Caudale". Caudale Beck flows from Caudale Moor into Kirkstone Beck, some 7 miles south - east of Patterdale.

# CARLISLE CLOSE

Originally intended to be called Kendal Close but probably changed to avoid confusion with "Candale".

# CARTMEL DRIVE

Village in the south part of Cumbria, 6 miles east of Ulverston. Before 1974 it was in north Lancashire.

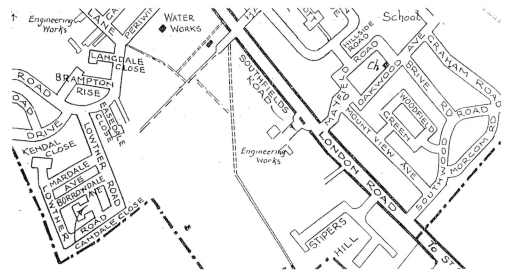

*An extract of the street map with the 1960 Town Guide which shows Carlisle Close as Kendal Close and also indicates the original intention that Lowther Road should extend into what is now Derwent Drive.*

## CROSBY CLOSE

Village 3 miles north-west of Maryport on the river Derwent. There are also two small hamlets called Crosby Ravensworth 4 miles south-west of Appleby and Crosby Garrett 6 miles south of the same town.

## DERWENT DRIVE

Derwent Water, a lake in the basin of the river Derwent (see Borrowdale) south of Keswick. Then it flows north-west through Bassenthwaite Lake, then west through Cockermouth to the sea at Workington. It is a common name in Britain as it means "River where the oaks are common". There are many other Derwents in Northumberland, Durham, Yorkshire and Derbyshire.

*Derwent Drive in 1999. (BS)*

## EASEDALE CLOSE

Small river descending from High White Stone, forming Easedale Tarn then flowing into Grasmere, 6 miles north-west of Ambleside.

# ENNERDALE AVENUE

Ennerdale Water the most westerly lake of the county, 6 miles east of Whitehaven of which it is the water provider.

# GRASMERE AVENUE

Village 1½ miles noth wset of Ambleside. The poet William Wordsworth lived in Dove Cottage there, which is preserved today. Wordsworth and his family are buried in the village churchyard. Grasmere is also a sheet of water 1mile long by 1½ miles broad.

# HILTON AVENUE

There are 20 Hilton villages in the Bartholomew Gazetteer of Britain, no wonder as it simply means "the settlement on the hill". The one in Cumbria is 3 miles east of Appleby.

# KESWICK CLOSE

Market town on the river Greta at the lower end of Derwent water. The town has long been famous for the manufacture of lead pencils.

# KIRKSTONE DRIVE

Kirkstone Pass, rocky mountain pass on the road between Ullswater and Windermere, 1500ft (455m). Near the summit, on the north side, some stones look like a church, probably explaining the origin of the name "Church Stone".

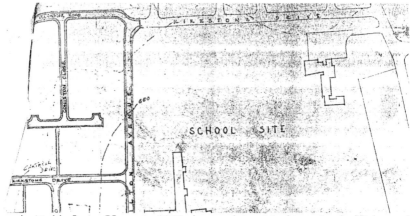

*Plans submitted by Laing Homes in 1960 showing their original intention for Kirkstone Drive to be extended into what is now Canesworde Road. Tarnside Close is also shown as Coniston Close.*

# LANGDALE CLOSE AND ROAD

Langdale Pikes, Langdale Fell, Great Langdale Beck and Little Langdale Tarn in the area north-west and west of Ambleside. At the heart of the Lake District, there are very few villages in the area.

*Langdale Road looking east from the junction with Kirkstone Drive in 1976. (AM)*

# LOWTHER ROAD

The road was originally designed as a crescent leading from Langdale Road and incorporating what is now Derwent Drive. However, following approval of William Old Ltd. to develop their Oldhill Down Estate, it was agreed between the parties that Lowther Road be extended as a link between the two estates. The Oldhill Estate did originally extend beyond the borders of Dunstable into Kensworth Parish and the Kensworth end of the estate was developed in parallel to the Dunstable section, the two "ends" of Lowther Road only being joined together some years after work first started. It is for this reason that the house numbers jump by 400 at the point of the former boundary. This part of Kensworth was eventually incorporated into Dunstable in April 1985.

The river Lowther flows north out of Haweswater before reaching Penrith where it joins River Eamont flowing from Ullswater. 4 miles south of Penrith, on the river, just inside the National Park there are Lowther Castle and Lowther Park.

*A letterhead of the original Developers, Martin Homes, showing their address in Lowther Road, Stanmore.*

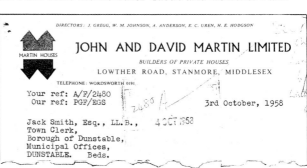

273

*The southern section of Lowther Road (nearest to Beech Road) under construction in 1966.(AR)*

## MARDALE AVENUE

Mardale Common and Mardale Bank are the names of mountainous areas situated at the south-east of Haweswater Reservoir, some 11 miles south of Penrith.

## MORLAND CLOSE

Attractive village in the Lyvennet valley, 6 miles north east of Appleby.

## PATTERDALE CLOSE

Village at the extreme south of Ullswater. It is a favourite place for the ascent of Helvellyn.

## PENRITH AVENUE

Market town on the River Eamont, 18 miles south east of Carlisle. On the Preston to Carlisle railway line.

## STAVELEY ROAD

Large village between Kendal and Windermere. Railway station.

## TARNSIDE CLOSE

On the first Estate plans submitted by Laing Homes in 1959 it is shown as "Coniston Close" but this name had disappeared a year later and I have found no evidence of why there was a change of heart. Tarnside is a hamlet 5 miles west-south-west of Kendal.

## ULLSWATER ROAD

The second largest lake in the county out of the north end. 5 miles from Penrith flows the River Eamont. It is $7\frac{1}{3}$ miles long from there to the extreme south end at Patterdale, a little less than $\frac{1}{2}$ mile broad on an average.

## ULVERSTON ROAD

Town in the south of the district, 8 miles north-east of Barrow-in-Furness. On the railway line from Lancaster to Barrow. Locally it is known as "Ooston".

## WINDERMERE CLOSE

The largest lake of the district. 10 ½ miles long, 1 mile broad. On the east shore is the touristic town of Windermere, terminus of the railway line from Kendal.

### The Oldhill Down Estate

William Old Ltd first submitted plans for a major new housing estate to extend southwards beyond the Laing's Croft Golf Course Estate. Construction started about a year later. Most of the roads on the estate refer to either noted buildings or locations near to Dunstable or to ancient field names. The few names which I have so far been unable to trace probably originate in one or other of these sources. In this section of the chapter I have included a few roads in the general locality even if they were not actually constructed as part of the original estate.

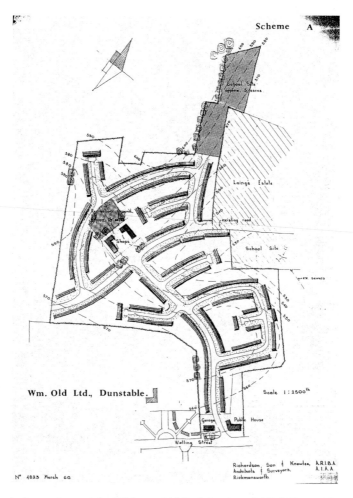

*The original plans submitted by William Old Ltd for their Oldhill Down Estate in March 1960.*

## ARDLEY CLOSE

Like Ardley Hill School based on the original field name for the area now comprising Kirkstone Drive/Staveley Road. The name is derived from the old English word "ardle" meaning hard, stony ground. The play area at the rear of these houses is the top of the original Ardley Hill.

## BOWLES WAY

Leslie Bowles was a long-serving Chairman of Bedfordshire County Council. I was told that it was on his casting vote that the decision was taken to implement comprehensive education in 1971, so sealing the fate of Dunstable Grammar School .

# BIBSHALL CRESCENT

According to Worthington Smith, an old local name, possibly Bibba's Hall. There is also a Bibshall Spring near Edlesborough.

*Looking west from the Bibshall Crescent/Oldhill junction in August 1971. In the background, the Lowther Road shops are under construction and West Hill is starting to be developed.(LM/DG)*

# BRIERLEY CLOSE

Other streets in this area refer to local place or field names but I have been unable to trace the origin of this particular road. However, "brier" is an altenative way of spelling briar so it could refer to an earlier field name.

# THE CHEVERALLS

Probably a mis-spelling of Cheverells Park near Markyate as most roads in this vicinity refer to locations near Dunstable. However, the road name coincides with the unusual spelling of a local family, the Cheverells. Mr Walter Cheverall ran a soft furnishing business in Queensway at the time the road was built. Mr Ian Cheverall of The Grange, Tebworth, confirms his branch of the family was originally spelt with three "e's" but was changed to Cheverall owing to a mis-spelling by the Army bureaucracy when his father, James, enlisted for the South African War in 1900.

*An advertisement for Cheveralls Furnishers in 1967.*

*Cheverells Park near Markyate.*   *Street party in the Cheveralls for the royal wedding of Charles and Diana in July 1981. (LM/DG)*

## CHURCHILL ROAD

Commemorates Sir Winston Spencer Churchill.

## FOXDELLS

An old field name on the north-west side of the present Kensworth Chalk Quarry.

## FURZON CLOSE

An old field name between Robertson Corner on Whipsnade Road and the east side of Kensworth Quarry. *Furze* is an alternative name for gorse which is common on rough pastures.

## GILDED ACRE

An old field name for a strip of land along the A5 between the present Oldhill and the footpath to Birchside.

## GROVEBURY CLOSE

Refers to Grovebury Manor ( and later Farmhouse) near Leighton Buzzard. The site of the even earlier Grove Priory was extensively excavated by Bedfordshire County Council during the 1980's.

*Grove Priory or Grovebury near Leighton Buzzard. View of the excavations looking east in 1978 showing monastic and later mediaeval manorial buildings. (BCC).*

279

## KNOTTS CLOSE

The present development is situated on part of an original two-acre field called Knotts Bushes on the pre-1907 parish map of Kensworth, in which it was then located.

## MAUNDSEY CLOSE

No suggestion.

## MENTMORE CRESCENT

This may refer to either Mentmore Towers, the Victorian Mansion of Baron Meyer de Rothschild near Leighton Buzzard or the Italian Restaurant at 26 Church Street which was previously known as "Mentmore House". When the row of cottages which used to stand to the east of this building were demolished in the 1960's, a local pressure group was successful in securing its preservation.

*A 1952 advertisement for Mentmore House.*

Antiques of all Periods bought and sold

ANTIQUES

W. RIXSON

LICENSED VALUER FOR PROBATE DUTY, ETC.

**William Rixson**

" Mentmore," Church Street, Dunstable, Beds.

Established since 1865          Telephone 27

76

## MILETREE CRESCENT

It has been suggested that a tree near this site was exactly one mile from the town centre crossroads, but I have been unable to find any direct evidence that this was so.

## OLDHILL

The main access road to the estate incorporates the Developers' name, William Old Ltd.

## TURNPIKE CLOSE

Remembers the Toll Gate or Turnpike which stood near the Half Moon Inn. It was originally erected at Turnpike Farm on Watling Street in 1723.

*A drawing of the Tollgate operated by the Turnpike Trust. It once stood south of Dunstable near to Turnpike Farm but was later moved to near Half Moon House in London Road. (BCC)*

*Turnpike Farm on Watling Street south of Dunstable.(BS)*

## VALENCE END

Could refer to Valence End Farm on Tring Road. The farm was called "Valenciennes" on the 19th century O.S. map.

*Valence End Farm at the foot of Bison Hill, Whipsnade in June 1999.(BS)*

## WAYSIDE

No suggestion.

## WESTHILL

A self defining name for a hill on the western boundary of the town.

### The Stipers Hill Estate

The original name for a 1930's development by the British Land Settlement Association which sought to provide cottage homesteads for unemployed workers in depressed areas of the country. Those settling in Dunstable came mainly from the North East and South Wales. The name comes from the original field name for the area. This part of Dunstable was originally in the parish of Kensworth and Kensworth historians, Malcolm and Irene Millest, have been told that it refers to a "stipe", a stalk in plants which bear reproductive structures especially the stalk bearing the cap of a mushroom. Apparently, some years ago the area of "Stipers Hill" was so named because of the long stemmed hallucinogenic mushrooms that grew there. The various roads on the estate were subsequently given individual names - see Lockhart, Garrett and Seamons (Birchside and Burges Close followed later).

Telephone: WHITEHALL 7612

Telegrams: LANSETTLER, SOWEST, LONDON

# THE LAND SETTLEMENT ASSOCIATION LTD.

Registered under the Industrial and Provident Societies Act 1893-1928

Chairman:
Sir PERCY R. JACKSON, J.P., LL.D.
Vice-Chairman:
A. C. RICHMOND.
Director and Secretary:
L. D. GAMMANS.

BROADWAY BUILDINGS,

BROADWAY, WESTMINSTER,

LONDON, S.W.1.

In your reply please quote .....C...35

11th July, 1938.

Dear Sir,

### Cottage Homesteads - Watling Street.

      The Cottage Homesteads Sub-Committee of this Association has had under consideration the various street names for our Cottage Homesteads scheme at Dunstable, and has now decided to act on your suggestion and incorporate the old name of Stipers Hill Close. It is felt, however, that in view of the fact that there is actually a Close included in the scheme the use of the full name might lead to confusion and we should therefore like to call the full scheme Stipers Hill and number the houses straight through, close and all included. I would be grateful if you would kindly put this proposal before your Highways Committee and seek their approval on our behalf.

      I should like to take this opportunity also of making formal application to your Council for the erection of the notice-board at the entrance to our estate indicating the name thereof.

              Yours very truly,

The Town Clerk,
Borough of Dunstable,
Town Clerk's Office,
DUNSTABLE,
Beds.
ENE/PJ

*A letter from the Land Settlement Association agreeing to the name "Stipers Hill".*

*An aerial view of the original Stipers Hill layout in 1947. What was later to become Burges Close and Birchside have yet to be developed. In the top of the picture the then cul-de-sac of Sundown Avenue is the only other development in the area. The Downside Estate would not be started for another five years .(RAF)*

# BIRCH SIDE

When the streets of the Stipers Hill Estate were individually named, all but this one commemorated past Mayors. I have been unable to find the reason for this particular name. Like its near neighbour, Beech Road, it may be named after the tree. Another possibility is that Birch is an old established Dunstable surname and may refer to some past member of that family.

*Birchside in March 1975. (BT)*

# BURGES CLOSE

Samuel Burges was one of the principal organisers of the 500 signature petition which led to the granting by Queen Victoria of the Dunstable Charter of Incorporation in 1864. He was elected Mayor of Dunstable in 1868.

*Councillor Samuel Burges in 1868.*

## GARRETT CLOSE

Fred Turner Garrett was one of the longest serving Mayors of Dunstable who was elected to the Town's highest office on 7 occasions between 1897 and 1919. A jeweller, he presented to the Council the Mayoral Chain of Office which is still worn regularly by Mayors today.

*A postcard showing the old Town Hall prepared for the Civic Banquet of Councillor and Mrs Fred Garrett in 1906.*

## LOCKHART CLOSE

The name was selected in 1968 to honour the local family who had been prominent in commercial life of the town for generations. Edward Lockhart was Mayor on three occasions in the 1870's and Percy William Lockhart was Mayor in 1928. A coal merchant and builders merchant he resided at "Cordova" in West Street, now the home of Dunstable Old People's Welfare Association.

*Councillor P W Lockhart being installed as Mayor of Dunstable in 1928 under the watchful gaze of the Town Clerk, Mr J M Coombes.*

# SEAMONS CLOSE

William Edwin Seamons, a nurseryman and florist in West Parade, was Mayor in 1920-21.

*Seamons Close in April 1975 before it was fully made up to highway adoption standards .(BT)*

## Other Streets

# ABBEY MEWS

Constructed by Abbeygate Developments in 1980. Alternative suggestions put forward by the Council but not accepted by the Developers were Augustine Court and Valley Court.

# BEECH ROAD/BEECH CLOSE

Likely origins as above. Beech Close was originally the site of Priory Hospital which in turn was originally the town's Isolation Hospital.

*Priory Hospital, Beech Road in October 1977. (LM/DG)*

THERE IS NO ACCIDENT SERVICE AT THIS HOSPITAL

THE NEAREST ACCIDENT AND EMERGENCY DEPARTMENT IS AT THE LUTON AND DUNSTABLE HOSPITAL ( JUST OFF THE JUNCTION OF A505 & M1.)

# BOWMANS WAY/CLOSE

This 1984 development by Connolly Homes was on the site of medieval archery practice grounds which were more recently the Dunstable Waterworks. The water tower remains a local Dunstable landmark.

*The Water Tower of Dunstable Waterworks in June 1968 seen from the vacant field which was later developed as Bowmans Way. (LM/DG)*

# BRITTANY COURT

Mr Charles Crow, the proprietor of Clarke's hardware, redeveloped his premises into this shopping parade and apparently he chose the name Brittany because the site was immediately opposite the entrance to Britain Street.

*Clarke's Hardware Stores in High Street South in April 1960 before the site was re-developed as Brittany Court.(BT)*

# BULL POND LANE

One of the oldest lanes in the town which once contained a pond located near the play area in what is now Bennett Memorial Recreation Ground. The 1822 Tithe Map shows the land south of the pond as "Bull Pond Piece".It is said that the lane led through the fields to a "Bull Rinc" or Pound which stood behind the Half Moon Inn.

*The Salvation Army Citadel which stood at the junction of Bull Pond Lane and St Mary's Street in 1970. The building was demolished to make way for the new Worship and Community Centre in 1993. (JB)*

*Bull Pond Lane in 1995. (SBDC)*

*An aerial view of First Avenue in 1938 showing homes still being developed. Bull Pond Lane is still an unmade track and in the*

# THE CEDARS

The Council rejected the Developers' suggestion in 1968 of "Cricket Place" (the site backed onto the former Dunstable Town Cricket Ground) and instead opted for this name which is taken from the large property on High Street South behind which the road was developed. This property, now a furniture showroom, still clearly displays the name "The Cedars".

# FIRST AVENUE

Prior to the Second World War, Kingcroft Estate laid out First Avenue for sale in building plots. Other avenues were also proposed and trees were planted in adjoining fields for this purpose and they struggled to survive for many years. The introduction of the Town and Country Planning Act in 1947 resulted in these fields being protected by post war planning concepts so Second Avenue, etc did not follow. The fields were, however, eventually developed in the early 1960's as part of the Laing's "Croft Golf Course Estate".

# FURNESS AVENUE

Two possibilities here. The development is on the site of the Harrison Carter Engineering Works and could therefore be a corruption of "furnace". Alternatively it could follow the general "lakeland" theme of the area and refer to Furness in Cumbria.

*A 1905 advertisement for Harrison Carter's Engineering Works.*

**J. HARRISON CARTER,**

London Office : **Engineering Works**
82, MARK LANE, E.C. **DUNSTABLE.**

Telegraphic Address : { " MILLING, DUNSTABLE." / " MILLING, LONDON."

**SOLE MAKER**
OF THE
**CARTER DISINTEGRATOR.**

Prices:
FROM
**£16**
TO
**£120.**

ADVANTAGES.
Compactness.
Cheapness.
Large Output.
Adaptability.
Low Up-keep.
Little Attention.
All Parts Hardened & Renewable.

Nº 2½
**WILL GRIND & DRESS ALMOST EVERY MATERIAL.**
Write to above Address for Catalogue.

ALSO MAKER OF ALL KINDS OF
**GRINDING, DRESSING, ELEVATING AND CONVEYING MACHINERY, PULLEYS, SHAFTING, CASTINGS.**
REPAIRS.
Visitors to the Town requiring Grinding Machinery, are invited to call and inspect the Works.

# GARDEN ROAD

First laid out in the 1890's, it has been suggested that the name refers to the site of gardens of houses in High Street South.

*A Coronation Street Party in Garden Road in June 1953. (BT)*

# GRAPHIC CLOSE

The graphic design department of Index Printers (see Index Way) stood on this site.

# HAWTHORN CLOSE

Constructed land originally forming part of Hawthorn Farm. The farm buildings were located on High Street South (see Staines Square). The Developer initially wished to call the street "Andrews Way" but the Council opposed this.

# HILLYFIELDS

Retains a local name for the area. A fine row of beech trees follows the line of the western half of the ancient Half Moon Lane.

# INDEX COURT/INDEX DRIVE

Housing Development on the site of the former Index Printing Works.

*Index Printing Works prior to demolition in April 1993. (DB)*

*Index Drive from the same viewpoint, July 1995. (DB)*

*Index Printing Works seen from London Road, April 1993. (DB)*

*Index Court from the same viewpoint, July 1995. (DB)*

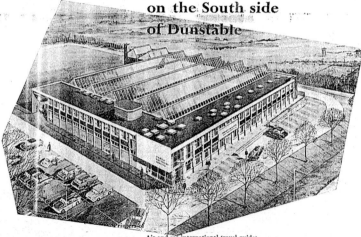

# INDEX
# PRINTERS
# LIMITED

this year

### still in Church Walk

## next year

### in this splendid new factory
### on the South side
### of Dunstable

Air and sea international travel guides
Rail, Coach and Bus timetables
Publications on Museums, Historic Houses, Castles and Gardens within U.K.
Road Haulage and Overseas Rail Systems

*A 1965 advertisement for the new Index Printing Works to be opened the following year.*

## KENSWORTH GATE

This office development in High Street South was originally proposed as "Watling Place" but this was thought to be confusing with the development of the same name in Houghton Regis and with Watling Court in High Street North. The site adjoins the original boundary of Dunstable with Kensworth Parish, then part of Hertfordshire.

# LONDON ROAD

The section of the A5 south of the 1909 borough boundary once known as Watling Street, was formally re-named London Road in 1933.

*That part of London Road known locally as Half Moon Hill about 1900 with the Half Moon Inn on the left.(BS)*

*An aerial view of London Road in 1968 showing the Empire Rubber Company (now BTR) in the foreground with the Downside Estate beyond. (LM/DG)*

## PERIWINKLE LANE

Blue Periwinkle flowers are said to have grown in the lane before it was made up as a public highway in 1903.

## REGENCY COURT

Probably a companion for Viceroy Court.

## ROYALE WALK

No suggestion.

*A view of Royale Walk and Regency Court (formerly the Dunstablians Rugby Ground) in 1992 from the Dunstable Town Cricket Ground, itself soon to be lost to housing (see Woolpack Close). (SBDC)*

## SOUTHFIELDS ROAD

Like its sister road, Northfields, an uninspired choice for a new Council housing development on fields in the south of the town constructed in 1937.

# STAINES SQUARE

Built on the site of Hawthorn Farm (142 High Street South) which was for generations in the ownership of the Staines family. The last occupant was Arthur Joseph Staines who died in 1952 and by whose will one of the farm paddocks was conveyed to Dunstable Cricket Club (see Woolpack Close).

*Staines Square in 1985.*
*(BCC)*

# TIBBETT CLOSE

Part of the new development on the site of Index Printing Works which was founded by local printers and publishers, the Tibbett Family.

*An aerial view of the Index Printing Works (in centre) in July 1968. In the foreground the Water Works (now Bowmans Way) is still undeveloped. In the top left hand corner the Downside Prefab Estate is just about to be demolished for the Apollo Close/Chichester Close developments. (Aerofilms)*

## VICEROY COURT

No suggestion.

*An aerial view of High Street South in 1972 showing the recently completed Viceroy Court in the foreground. (Aerofilms)*

## WILLOUGHBY CLOSE

The town's latest housing development built on the site of Cross Paperware, retains the original field name for the area before the factory development. An alternative suggestion that at least part of the site be named "Doyley Close" to remember the paper doyleys for which Cross's were famous, did not find favour with the Developers.

*The Dunstable Pound just beyond the town boundary in London Road in about 1900. The site was soon to be developed as part of the Cross works. The lane on the right led to Kensworth and was once used as a means of avoiding the tolls payable for travelling on Watling Street (see Turnpike Close). (DG)*

*The Cross Paperware Factory in about 1900.*

## WOOLPACK CLOSE

Former Dunstable Cricket Ground. The two fields which originally comprised this site were known as "Great Woolpack" and "Little Woolpack" and were at the rear of a public house of the same name in High Street South.

*The official opening of Dunstable Town Cricket Ground (now Woolpack Close) in 1950.*
*(DG)*

299

# Photograph Acknowledgements

The kind permission of the following to reproduce photographs is gratefully acknowledged:

| | | | |
|---|---|---|---|
| AM | Alan Moorhouse | LM | Luton Museum Service |
| AR | Ann Read | MAS | Manshead Archaeological Society of Dunstable |
| AW | The Arnold White Group | | |
| BCC | Beds County Council | MD | Mary Dolman |
| BS | Bill Stevens | MP | Mike Pierce |
| BT | Bruce Turvey | MT | Mary Townsend |
| DB | David Bunker | OM | Omer Roucoux |
| DG | The Dunstable Gazette | PH | Philip Heley |
| JB | The late John Branham (courtesy Dunstable and district Local History Society) | RAF | RAF photo by kind permission of the Ministry of Defence |
| JH | Jon Hitchcock | SBDC | South Bedfordshire District Council |
| JS | Joan Schneider | | |
| HM | Harry Maughan | VM | Vauxhall Motors Ltd |

All other photographs and documents are reproduced by kind permission of Dunstable Town Council.

## Street Maps

All current street maps in this publication are reproduced by kind permission of the Local Authority Publishing Co. Ltd.

## General Acknowledgements

I am extremely grateful to the following persons for the help and information they have provided during my researches into this subject:

Eric Baldock, Norman Bates, Bob Beasant, Bedfordshire and Luton Record Office, Colin Bourne, John Buckledee, Eric Bullock, Twink Bunker, Sam Caen, Peter Cheshire, The Dunstable Gazette, Vivienne Evans, Peter Flory, Chris Grabham, Terry Headey, Trevor Jones, Luton Museum Service, Ben Lee, Andy Lewis, John Lunn, Douglas Mead, Irene and Malcolm Millest, Fred Moore, Mary Owens, Omer Roucoux, Joan Schneider, Jack Smith, John Spurgeon, Bernard Stevens, Betty Tarbox, Wilf Turquand, Bruce Turvey, Colin White, Trevor Wood and last,but by no means least, my colleagues at Dunstable Town Council.

# STREET INDEX

Abbey Mews 287
Aidans Close 167
Albert Court 137
Albion Street 101
Aldbanks 168
Alfred Street 138
Allen Close 139
Allenby Avenue 234
Apex Business Centre 255
Apollo Close 140
Appleby Gardens 269
Ardley Close 276
Arnold Court 212
Ash Grove 156
Ashcroft 168
Ashton Road 192
Ashton Square 71
Avenue The 212
Aynscombe Close 169

Badgers Gate 213
Barley Brow 192
Barrie Avenue 192
Barton Avenue 141
Beacon Avenue 213
Beale Street 103
Beech Green 170
Beech Road/Beech Close 287
Beechwood Court 171
Beecroft Way 172
Bennetts Close 104
Benning Avenue 175
Bernard Close 74
Bibshall Crescent 277
Bigthan Road 142
Birchside 285
Blows Road 144
Borough Road 145
Borrowdale Avenue 269

Boscombe Road 256
Bowland Crescent 269
Bowles Way 276
Bowmans Way/Close 288
Brampton Rise 269
Brandreth Avenue 234
Brewers Hill Road 176
Brierley Close 277
Britain Street 144
Brittany Court 288
Brive Road 146
Broadwalk 74
Bryony Way 179
Buckwood Avenue 234
Bull Pond Lane 289
Bunhill Close 179
Bunkers Court 105
Burges Close 285
Burr Street 105
Buttercup Close 107
Buttermere Avenue 270

Calcutt Close 234
Campion Close 179
Candale Close 270
Canesworde Road 107
Capron Road 197
Carlisle Close 270
Carterweys 235
Cartmel Drive 270
Catchacre 108
Cedars The 291
Cemetery Lane 109
Chadwick Close 109
Chapel Walk 75
Cheveralls The 277
Cheyne Close 198
Chichester Close 148
Chiltern Court 110

| | | | | |
|---|---|---|---|---|
| Chiltern Park | 260 | Fairfield Close/Road | 237 |
| Chiltern Road | 111 | Falcon Close | 205 |
| Church Close | 66 | First Avenue | 291 |
| Church Street | 58 | Flint Court | 118 |
| Church Walk | 69 | Foxdell | 276 |
| Churchhill Road | 278 | Franklin Road | 183 |
| Clifton Road | 113 | French's Avenue | 198 |
| Cookfield Close | 179 | Friars Walk and Friary | 81 |
| Coombe Drive | 214 | Field | |
| Court Drive | 77 | Furness Avenue | 291 |
| Crabtree Way | 205 | Furzon Close | 279 |
| Creasey Park Drive | 179 | | |
| Crest The | 253 | Garden Road | 292 |
| Cresta Close | 236 | Gardeners Close | 215 |
| Croft Green | 180 | Garrett Close | 286 |
| Crosby Close | 271 | George Street | 199 |
| Cross Street North | 114 | Gilded Acre | 279 |
| Cusworth Way/Walk | 167 | Gilpin Chase/Street | 201 |
| | | Goldstone Crescent | 237 |
| Dale Close/Road | 236 | Gorham Way | 238 |
| Derwent Drive | 271 | Graham Road | 151 |
| Dog Kennel Walk (or | 79 | Graphic Close | 292 |
| Path) | | Grasmere Close | 272 |
| Dorchester Close | 80 | Great Northern Road | 152 |
| Douglas Crescent | 198 | Greenfield Close | 184 |
| Downs Road | 148 | Green Lanes | 215 |
| Drakes Court | 148 | Grove Road | 153 |
| Drovers Way | 181 | Grovebury Close | 279 |
| Dukeminster Estate | 260 | | |
| Duncombe Drive | 236 | Hadrian Avenue | 238 |
| Dunstable Road | 214 | Half Moon Lane | 154 |
| | | Hambling Place | 184 |
| Easedale Close | 271 | Harvey Road | 215 |
| Eastern Avenue | 262 | Hawthorn Close | 292 |
| Edward Street | 114 | High Street North | 22 |
| Eleanor's Cross | 117 | High Street South | 37 |
| Elizabeth Court | 149 | Highfields Court | 239 |
| England's Avenue | 199 | Hillcroft | 185 |
| England's Lane | 150 | Hillside Road | 155 |
| Ennerdale Avenue | 272 | Hillyfields | 292 |
| Evelyn Road | 237 | Hilton Avenue | 272 |

| | | | | |
|---|---|---|---|---|
| Holland Court | 155 | Linden Road and Close | 244 |
| Holliwicke Road | 239 | Liscombe Road | 244 |
| Holmwood Close | 240 | Lockhart Close | 286 |
| Holts Court | 118 | Lockington Crescent | 246 |
| Houghton Parade | 201 | London Road | 295 |
| Houghton Road | 202 | Long Hedge | 256 |
| Howard Place | 155 | Long Meadow | 119 |
| Hurlock Close | 216 | Loring Road | 185 |
| | | Lovers Walk | 157 |
| Icknield Street | 83 | Lovett Way | 265 |
| Icknield Villas | 83 | Lowther Road | 273 |
| Index Court/Index Drive | 292 | Ludun Close | 246 |
| Ivy Close | 179 | Luton Road | 247 |
| | | | |
| Jardine Way | 155 | Maidenbower Avenue | 186 |
| Jeansway | 240 | Mall The | 88 |
| | | Maltings The | 131 |
| Katherine Drive | 240 | Manchester Place | 119 |
| Kensworth Gate | 294 | Manshead Court | 157 |
| Keswick Close | 272 | Mardale Avenue | 274 |
| King Street | 156 | Marina Drive | 217 |
| Kingsbury Avenue and | 243 | Markham Crescent | 249 |
| Gardens | | Matthew Street | 121 |
| Kingsbury Court | 87 | Maundsey Close | 280 |
| Kingscroft Avenue | 88 | Mayfield Road | 157 |
| Kingsway | 84 | Maypole Yard | 121 |
| Kirby Road | 119 | Meadway | 218 |
| Kirkstone Drive | 272 | Melton Court | 220 |
| Knotts Close | 280 | Mentmore Crescent | 280 |
| | | Middle Row | 89 |
| Lambs Close | 243 | Miletree Crescent | 280 |
| Lancot Avenue | 216 | Millers Ley | 250 |
| Lancot Drive | 217 | Monks Close | 250 |
| Langdale Close and Road | 273 | Morcom Road | 158 |
| Langridge Court | 185 | Morland Close | 274 |
| Laurelside Walk | | Mountview Avenue | 159 |
| Lawns The | 98 | | |
| Lawrence Way | 185 | New Woodfield Green | 160 |
| Leighton Court | 119 | Nicholas Way | 90 |
| Leston Close | | Norcott Close | 161 |
| Lime Walk | 156 | Norman Way | 187 |
| Lincoln Close | 156 | | |

| | | | | |
|---|---|---|---|---|
| North Station Way | 187 | Ridgeway Avenue/Drive | 252 |
| Northfields | 203 | Rotherwood Close | 167 |
| Norton Court | 91 | Royale Walk | 296 |
| Nursery Close | 122 | Royce Close | 223 |
| | | | |
| Oak Close | 156 | Salters Way | 209 |
| Oakwell Close | 221 | Sandland Close | 126 |
| Oakwood Avenue | 159 | Saxon Close | 189 |
| Oldhill | 281 | Scawsby Close | 167 |
| Olma Road | 204 | Scott Court | 96 |
| Orchid Close | 189 | Seamons Close | 286 |
| Osborne Road | 123 | Sheridan Close | 205 |
| | | Skimpot Road | 253 |
| Palma Close | 204 | Southfields Road | 296 |
| Park Road | 161 | Southwood Road | 164 |
| Park Street | 204 | Spinney Crescent | 190 |
| Parrott Close | 250 | Spoondell | 226 |
| Pascomb Road | 189 | Square The | 45 |
| Patterdale Close | 274 | St Christopher's Close | 252 |
| Penrith Avenue | 274 | St Mary's Gate | 96 |
| Periwinkle Lane | 296 | St Peter's Road | 163 |
| Pipers Croft | 221 | Staines Square | 297 |
| Porz Avenue | 263 | Station Road | 165 |
| Poynters Road | 251 | Staveley Road | 275 |
| Primrose Court | 123 | Stewart Clarke Court | 127 |
| Princes Street | 124 | Stipers Hill | 282 |
| Printers Way | 205 | Stuart Street | 127 |
| Priory Road | 161 | Suffolk Close | 166 |
| Pynders Lane | 252 | Sugden Court | 128 |
| | | Sunbower Avenue | 210 |
| Quadrant The | 91 | Suncote Avenue | 210 |
| Queens Court | 209 | Sundown Avenue | 166 |
| Queensway | 93 | Swan Court | 128 |
| | | | |
| Radburn Court | 125 | Tarnside Close | 275 |
| Ravenscourt | 209 | Tavistock Street | 210 |
| Readers Close | 205 | Thornbury | 253 |
| Redfield Close | 189 | Tibbett Close | 297 |
| Regency Court | 296 | Totternhoe Road | 226 |
| Regent Street | 125 | Tring Road | 228 |
| Retreat The | 253 | Turnpike Close | 281 |
| Richard Street | 163 | | |

| | |
|---|---|
| Ullswater Road | 275 |
| Ulverston Road | 275 |
| Union Street | 129 |
| | |
| Valence End | 282 |
| Verey Road | 265 |
| Vernon Place | 99 |
| Viceroy Court | 298 |
| Victoria Street | 131 |
| | |
| Walgrave Road | 253 |
| Waterlow Road | 133 |
| Watling Court | 210 |
| Wayside | 282 |
| Weatherby | 190 |
| Wellington Terrace | 166 |
| West Parade | 134 |
| West Street | 51 |
| Westdown Gardens | 229 |
| Western Way | 254 |
| Westfield Road | 191 |
| Westhill | 282 |
| Whipsnade Road | 231 |
| Wilbury Drive | 254 |
| Willoughby Close | 298 |
| Windermere Close | 275 |
| Winfield Street | 135 |
| Wingate Road | 254 |
| Wood Street | 100 |
| Woodfield Gate | 166 |
| Woodford Road | 254 |
| Woolpack Close | 299 |
| Worthington Road | 192 |

# Subscribers

Mrs A P Abbiss

Percy Allen

Anne Allsopp

Rosemary & Dan Bateman

Mr & Mrs R W Billett

Tony & Hilary Blake

Brenda & Peter Boatwright

Mr T P Bowers

Gary Bracken

Kevin A Brigginshaw

Mrs Ann P Buchanan

E Bullock

Laura & Joe Burgess

N S T Caller

P J Campion

Mr J L & Mrs L R Carey

Marjory Carter

Steve Carvell

Brian Chapman

Mr & Mrs John Chernowski

Mr & Mrs Paul Chernowski

Barbara & David Cheshire

Mrs B Clarke

Doreen Cole

Mrs Josephine Colver

Ealey D Conquest

Jim & Vera Cook

Mr E G C Cook

B J Cope

Mrs Anne Cross

Mrs Joan Curran

Mrs Margaret Curry

Dr & Mrs N E Curt & Family

Christopher R Day

W & M Dewar

J G & L M Dickin

Christopher & Sarah Doe

Eric G Duncombe

Dunstable & District Local History Society

Myrtle Etherington

Robert Etherington

Mr R S & Mrs U M Eustace

Vivienne & Lewis Evans

Victoria Faulkner

Miss M J Field & Mr & Mrs F A Bird

Anthony Field

Councillor Reg & Joan Fossey JP

Mr & Mrs R Frith

Hugh Garrod

Mrs S Glendinning

Tony & Barbara Harris

Cecilia & Peter Hart

Leonard & Jennifer Haynes

Mrs V Heley

Mr T J Holloway

Tony C Horn

Mrs K M Horne

Richard A Horne

Jim & Jacqui Hunt

Paul Hunt

Mr & Mrs J & Y R Hutt

Mr Raymond Jackson

Ena & Aubrey Jones

Mr Stephen Kane

Pauline Keen

Mr & Mrs King

Mr & Mrs S Knight

Sally & Terry Layton

Mr J M W Liberty

David Lindsey

Margaret & Roy Lines

Mrs P Lovering

Mrs N M Luff

John Lunn MBE

Patricia & David Lye

Les Marsh

Cliff & Lyn Martin

Mr & Mrs D Maskell

Mr Harry Maughan
A W & P S Morgan
Bill Morgan
Peter Munro
Mrs S E Nash
Mrs Pauline Neill
Martin North
John O'Brien
Miss E Odell
Ken Owen
Mary Owen
Wendy & Peter Parker
R B Pepworth
Malcolm & Jean Phillip
Trevor & Helen Pocock
Elisabeth Pynn
Geoff & June Rawson
C Read
Mrs C L Reeve
Steven Paul Rennison
Tom & Ann Renwick
Peter & Susan Revell
Vivien Rix
C W Rogers
C D Rogers
R C Rogers
David Room
Jean M Sands
Joan Schneider
Mr C G & Mrs A L Sieling
Christine Sinfield

Mr & Mrs Robert Charles Smith
Mrs P Smith
Derek & June Sparrow
Jason Sparrow
Aubrey Stanbridge
Bernard Stevens
Councillor W J Stevens
Mr & Mrs J B Stevens
Tim Stevens
Matthew Street
Maralyne Syratt
Allan & Betty Thompson
Councillor Mike Tilley JP
Brandon & Lana Tookey
Mary Townsend
Mr & Mrs P Tucker
J T Tyler
Mrs Vera Volpe
David Waldock
Joshua Waldock
Lois Waldock
Mark Waldock
Norman & Beverly Waldock
Sharon Waldock
Anthony J Ward
Wendy Watson
Dave West
Mary Whitman
Paul Whitten
Ian Whyte
Derek, Elaine, Verity & Trudie Woolhead

**An overview of Dunstable's dramatic history
through the last millennium ...**

# PROUD HERITAGE

## A Brief History of Dunstable, 1000–2000AD

**Vivienne Evans**

Sited on a crossroads less than forty miles from London, Oxford and Cambridge, century by century Dunstable has been involved in many national events. Its populace has had to face economic and religious upheavals, but time after time Dunstablians have pulled together, changed direction and won through to another successful era.

Devoting a chapter to each of the ten centuries of the millennium, this book first sets the national and county scene in order to make more comprehensible the purely Dunstable events. This is a town of rich tradition and amazing happenings – all in all one which can be said to have enjoyed a heritage of which we can all still be truly proud.

# DUNSTABLE
# WITH THE PRIORY, 1100–1550

## Vivienne Evans

Soon after 1100 Henry I's advisers planted a market town, of experienced businessmen, on the corner of his 'household manor', Houghton Regis. A royal palace was added and a few years later Henry invited a house of Augustinian Canons from London to build a new Priory opposite. In due course a rival monastery, a Dominican Friary, was also established in the town. However it took some years for businessmen and monks to learn to work together and their struggle for supremacy was often stormy.

Throughout the period up to 1550, Dunstable played an important role in national life – for example, its involvement in Magna Carta and the Peasants' Revolt. Nearly every king and queen of England stayed in the town, whilst the annulment in the Priory of Henry VIII's marriage led to the foundation of the Anglican Church.

The town's site on the crossing of the famous Watling Street and Icknield Way was of crucial signficance and fame. A commemorative cross was erected there to mark the nearby overnight resting-place of the body of Edward I's Queen Eleanor; and its strategic advantages contributed to Dunstable's rapid rise to be one of the most successful new towns in the country during this period.

# DUNSTABLE
# IN TRANSITION, 1550 –1700

## Vivienne Evans

Following the sudden closure of the Augustinian Priory in the mid-sixteenth century, Dunstable's businessmen, retailers, traders and commuters needed to work together for change and eventually effected a very successful recovery.

Then came the Civil War and all groups suffered finanicial loss and some individuals serious distress. However, once the war was over, travellers started to pass through the town and the people took every opportunity to build up new businesses and to turn Dunstable into one of the leading travel centres between London and Holyhead.

Situated on two main roads they were in an excellent position to exploit this vibrant new industry. However, it also meant that they were exposed to the gossip, sedition, discussions and secret meetings which took place. The fate of kings, bishops and the Church of England were argued about in Dunstable's many inns. So it is not surprising that a second theme weaves in and out of these chapters; the struggle for freedom of worship. Some of the first Baptists in this country were a breakaway movement from the Priory Church of St. Peter and the early Quakers were welcomed at a house near the crossroads.

The 17th century has been described as 'a century of change' and Dunstable was at the centre of these enormous upheavals. This book opens to an uncertain future, covers the hardships and distress of war, follows the story of the town's newly-found prosperity and leaves it on the brink of even greater success and security.

# Books Published by
# THE BOOK CASTLE

**COUNTRYSIDE CYCLING IN BEDFORDSHIRE,
BUCKINGHAMSHIRE AND HERTFORDSHIRE**:  Mick Payne.
Twenty rides on- and off-road for all the family.

**PUB WALKS FROM COUNTRY STATIONS:
Bedfordshire and Hertfordshire**: Clive Higgs.
Fourteen circular country rambles, each starting and finishing at a railway
station and incorporating a pub-stop at a mid-way point.

**PUB WALKS FROM COUNTRY STATIONS:
Buckinghamshire and Oxfordshire:** Clive Higgs.
Circular rambles incorporating pub-stops.

**LOCAL WALKS: South Bedfordshire and North Chilterns:** Vaughan Basham.
Twenty-seven thematic circular walks.

**LOCAL WALKS: North and Mid Bedfordshire**: Vaughan Basham.
Twenty-five thematic circular walks.

**FAMILY WALKS: Chilterns South**: Nick Moon.
Thirty 3 to 5 mile circular walks.

**FAMILY WALKS: Chilterns North**: Nick Moon.
Thirty shorter circular walks.

**CHILTERN WALKS: Hertfordshire, Bedfordshire and
North Buckinghamshire**: Nick Moon.
**CHILTERN WALKS: Buckinghamshire**: Nick Moon.
**CHILTERN WALKS: Oxfordshire and
West Buckinghamshire**: Nick Moon.
A trilogy of circular walks, in association with the Chiltern Society.
Each volume contains 30 circular walks.

**OXFORDSHIRE WALKS: Oxford, the Cotswolds and the
Cherwell Valley**: Nick Moon.
**OXFORDSHIRE WALKS: Oxford, the Downs and
the Thames Valley**: Nick Moon.
Two volumes that complement Chiltern Walks: Oxfordshire and complete
coverage of the county, in association with the Oxford Fieldpaths Society.
Thirty circular walks in each.

**THE D'ARCY DALTON WAY**: Nick Moon.
Long-distance footpath across the Oxfordshire Cotswolds and Thames Valley,
with various circular walk suggestions.

**JOURNEYS INTO BEDFORDSHIRE**: Anthony Mackay.
Foreword by The Marquess of Tavistock, Woburn Abbey. A lavish book of over 150 evocative ink drawings.

**JOURNEYS INTO BUCKINGHAMSHIRE**: Anthony Mackay
Superb line drawings plus background text: large format landscape gift book.

**BUCKINGHAMSHIRE MURDERS**: Len Woodley
Nearly two centuries of nasty crimes.

**WINGRAVE: A Rothschild Village in the Vale**: Margaret and Ken Morley.
Thoroughly researched and copiously illustrated survey of the last 200 years in this lovely village between Aylesbury and Leighton Buzzard.

**HISTORIC FIGURES IN THE BUCKINGHAMSHIRE LANDSCAPE**:
John Houghton.
Major personalities and events that have shaped the county's past, including a special section on Bletchley Park.

**TWICE UPON A TIME**: John Houghton.
Short stories loosely based on fact, set in the North Bucks area.

**MANORS and MAYHEM, PAUPERS and PARSONS:**
**Tales from Four Shires: Beds., Bucks., Herts., and Northants.**: John Houghton
Little-known historical snippets and stories.

**MYTHS and WITCHES, PEOPLE and POLITICS:**
**Tales from Four Shires: Bucks., Beds., Herts., and Northants.**: John Houghton.
Anthology of strange, but true historical events.

**FOLK: Characters and Events in the History of Bedfordshire and Northamptonshire**: Vivienne Evans.
Anthology about people of yesteryear – arranged alphabetically by village or town.

**JOHN BUNYAN: His Life and Times**: Vivienne Evans.
Highly-praised and readable account.

**THE RAILWAY AGE IN BEDFORDSHIRE**: Fred Cockman.
Classic, illustrated account of early railway history.

**A LASTING IMPRESSION**: Michael Dundrow.
A boyhood evacuee recalls his years in the Chiltern village of Totternhoe near Dunstable.

**GLEANINGS REVISITED:**
**Nostalgic Thoughts of a Bedfordshire Farmer's Boy**: E W O'Dell.
His own sketches and early photographs adorn this lively account of rural Bedfordshire in days gone by.

**BEDFORDSHIRE'S YESTERYEARS Vol 2:**
**The Rural Scene**: Brenda Fraser-Newstead.
Vivid first-hand accounts of country life two or three generations ago.

**BEDFORDSHIRE'S YESTERYEARS Vol 3:**
**Craftsmen and Tradespeople**: Brenda Fraser-Newstead.
Fascinating recollections over several generations practising many vanishing crafts and trades.

**BEDFORDSHIRE'S YESTERYEARS Vol 4:**
**War Times and Civil Matters:** Brenda Fraser-Newstead.
Two World Wars, plus transport, law and order, etc.

**PROUD HERITAGE: A Brief History of Dunstable, 1000–2000AD:**
Vivienne Evans.
Century by century account of the town's rich tradition and key events, many of national significance.

**DUNSTABLE WITH THE PRIORY: 1100–1550**: Vivienne Evans.
Dramatic growth of Henry I's important new town around a major crossroads.

**DUNSTABLE IN TRANSITION: 1550–1700:**
Vivienne Evans.
Wealth of original material as the town evolves without the Priory.

**DUNSTABLE DECADE: THE EIGHTIES:**
**A Collection of Photographs**: Pat Lovering.
A souvenir book of nearly 300 pictures of people and events in the 1980s.

**STREETS AHEAD: An Illustrated Guide to the Origins of**
**Dunstable's Street Names**: Richard Walden.
Fascinating text and captions to hundreds of photographs, past and present, throughout the town.

**DUNSTABLE IN DETAIL**: Nigel Benson.
A hundred of the town's buildings and features, plus town trail map.

**OLD DUNSTABLE**: Bill Twaddle.
A new edition of this collection of early photographs.

**BOURNE and BRED: A Dunstable Boyhood Between the Wars:** Colin Bourne.
An elegantly written, well-illustrated book capturing the spirit of the town over fifty years ago.

**ROYAL HOUGHTON**: Pat Lovering:
Illustrated history of Houghton Regis from the earliest times to the present.

**THE STOPSLEY BOOK**: James Dyer.
Definitive, detailed account of this historic area of Luton. 150 rare photographs.

**THE STOPSLEY PICTURE BOOK**: James Dyer.
New material and photographs make an ideal companion to The Stopsley Book.

**PUBS and PINTS:**
**The Story of Luton's Public Houses and Breweries**: Stuart Smith.
The background to beer in the town, plus hundreds of photographs, old and new.

**THE CHANGING FACE OF LUTON: An Illustrated History**:
Stephen Bunker, Robin Holgate and Marian Nichols.
Luton's development from earliest times to the present busy industrial town.
Illustrated in colour and mono.

**WHERE THEY BURNT THE TOWN HALL DOWN:**
**Luton, The First World War and the Peace Day Riots, July 1919:** Dave Craddock.
Detailed analysis of a notorious incident.

**THE MEN WHO WORE STRAW HELMETS:**
**Policing Luton, 1840–1974:** Tom Madigan.
Meticulously chronicled history; dozens of rare photographs; author served in
Luton Police for fifty years.

**BETWEEN THE HILLS:**
**The Story of Lilley, a Chiltern Village:** Roy Pinnock.
A priceless piece of our heritage – the rural beauty remains but the customs and
way of life described here have largely disappeared.

**KENILWORTH SUNSET:**
**A Luton Town Supporter's Journal:** Tim Kingston.
Frank and funny account of football's ups and downs.

**A HATTER GOES MAD!**: Kristina Howells.
Luton Town footballers, officials and supporters talk to a female fan.

**LEGACIES:**
**Tales and Legends of Luton and the North Chilterns**: Vic Lea.
Twenty-five mysteries and stories based on fact, including Luton Town
Football Club. Many photographs.

**THREADS OF TIME**: Shela Porter.
The life of a remarkable mother and businesswoman, spanning the entire
century and based in Hitchin and (mainly) Bedford.

**LEAFING THROUGH LITERATURE:**
**Writers' Lives in Hertfordshire and Bedfordshire**: David Carroll.
Illustrated short biographies of many famous authors and their connections with
these counties.

**A PILGRIMAGE IN HERTFORDSHIRE**: H M Alderman.
Classic, between-the-wars tour round the county, embellished with line drawings.

**THE VALE OF THE NIGHTINGALE**: Molly Andrews.
Several generations of a family, lived against a Harpenden backdrop.

**SUGAR MICE AND STICKLEBACKS:**
**Childhood Memories of a Hertfordshire Lad**: Harry Edwards
Vivid evocation of those gentler pre-war days in an archetypal village,
Hertingfordbury.

**SWANS IN MY KITCHEN**: Lis Dorer.
Story of a Swan Sanctuary near Hemel Hempstead.

**THE HILL OF THE MARTYR:**
**An Architectural History of St. Albans Abbey**: Eileen Roberts.
Scholarly and readable chronological narrative history of Hertfordshire and
Bedfordshire's famous cathedral. Fully illustrated with photographs and plans.

**CHILTERN ARCHAEOLOGY: RECENT WORK:**
**A Handbook for the Next Decade**: edited by Robin Holgate.
The latest views, results and excavations by twenty-three leading archaeologists
throughout the Chilterns.

**THE TALL HITCHIN INSPECTOR'S CASEBOOK:**
**A Victorian Crime Novel Based on Fact**: Edgar Newman.
Worthies of the time encounter more archetypal villains.

# SPECIALLY FOR CHILDREN

**VILLA BELOW THE KNOLLS: A Story of Roman Britain**:
Michael Dundrow.
An exciting adventure for young John in Totternhoe and Dunstable two
thousand years ago.

**THE RAVENS: One Boy Against the Might of Rome**: James Dyer.
On the Barton Hills and in the south-east of England as the men of the great
fort of Ravensburgh (near Hexton) confront the invaders.

---

## Books Distributed by THE BOOK CASTLE

| | |
|---|---|
| Pictorial Guide to Bedfordshire | Meadows / Larkman |
| The Story of Bedford | Godber |
| Pictorial Guide to Hertfordshire | Meadows |
| The Story of St. Albans | Toms |
| History of Milton Keynes, vol 1 | Markham |
| History of Milton Keynes, vol 2 | Markham |
| Old Aylesbury | Viney / Nightingale |
| Village Schooldays and Beyond, 1906–23 | Chapman |
| Claydon | Chapman |

---

Further titles are in preparation.
All the above are available via any bookshop, or from the publisher and bookseller,
**THE BOOK CASTLE**
**12 Church Street Dunstable, Bedfordshire, LU5 4RU**
**Tel: (01582) 605670**